Tales from
Choteau Montana

The remarkable people, weather, crimes and events that made the local weekly news.

Also by Nancy C. Thornton

Tales from
Montana's Rocky Mountain Front

Tales from Montana's Teton County

Tales from Choteau Montana

The remarkable people, weather, crimes and events that made the local weekly news.

Nancy C. Thornton

Canal Heritage Enterprises
Choteau, Montana
2020

Cover Design: Ralph Thornton.
Front Cover: Choteau's Golden Rule Co. store, circa 1920s, in the McDonald Block building. Inset photograph: East side of Main Avenue, circa early 1900s. Unknown photographers. Digital copies retrieved from the Choteau Centennial Committee archives. Official map of Choteau, Montana, 1913 – 1985.

Back Cover: Sunrise over the plains, Copyright Ralph Thornton 2016. Inset photograph: Teton County Montana Courthouse, Copyright Nancy C. Thornton 2006. Inset photograph of the author, Copyright Nancy C. Thornton 2019.

The stories for this volume were written by Nancy C. Thornton and were originally published in the Choteau Acantha weekly newspaper. This volume has minor edits in the text for clarity. Grateful acknowledgment is made to the Choteau Acantha for permission to use copyrighted material.

First Printing: 2020

ISBN 978-0-9700704-5-6

Canal Heritage Enterprises
P.O. Box 1482
Choteau MT 59422
www.canalheritage.com

Contents

Acknowledgements

I would like to thank the Choteau Acantha publishers, Jeff and Melody Martinsen, and my husband, Ralph Thornton, without whose help this book would never have been completed.

Preface

"The newspapers are full of what we would like to happen to us and what we hope will never happen to us." — John Fowles

My interest in local history was honed by spending more than 25 years living near the small community of Lemont, Illinois, in the Illinois and Michigan Canal National Heritage Corridor, a narrowly-defined geographic area with a rich history and a few century-old local newspapers that documented that history.

After moving to Choteau, Montana, with my husband, Ralph, in 1999, I became intrigued by that same intensely local focus that the Choteau Acantha newspaper brought to its readers. I became a subscriber to and an employee of the Acantha.

The Choteau Acantha's "local news" focus is and always has been a paramount goal of its succession of publishers and editors since 1894. And so, the merging of my interest in the local history of the Rocky Mountain Front, Teton County and its county seat of Choteau naturally developed after reading the old newspapers of the region. They memorialize the history of the communities along the Front as does no other resource.

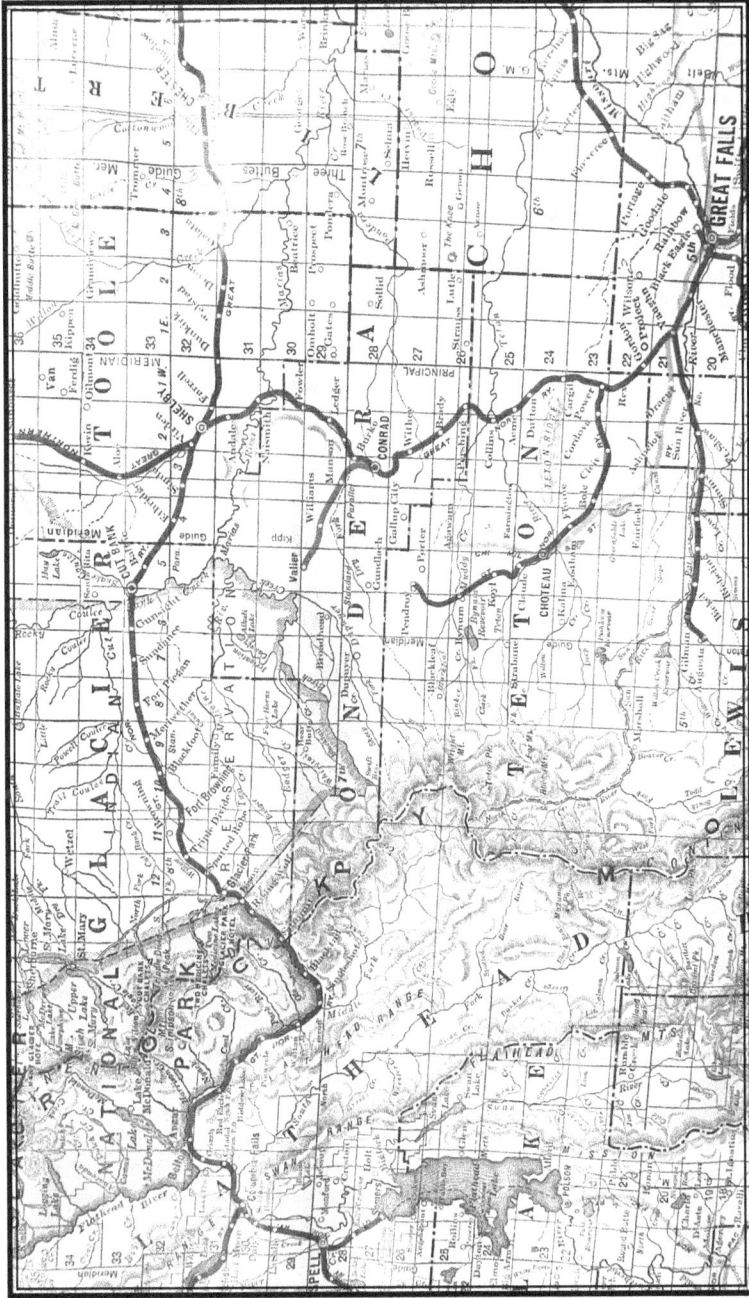

Map of the Great Northern Railway circa 1923. Source: Havre Railway Museum collection, 2018.

Introduction

In December 1883 post traders Alfred Hamilton and Isaac Hazlett filed the town plat of Choteau, Montana, in the valley of the Teton River about 20 miles from the Rocky Mountain Front.

"It is quite a pretentious looking city — on paper — and is likely to become such in fact. There are 19 blocks in the townsite with 28 lots to a block, the dimensions of the lots being 25x150 feet," the River Press in Fort Benton reported in 1883.

Before the entrepreneurs filed the plat, Choteau was named Old Agency, a reference to the Blackfeet Agency that operated from 1869 to 1876 three miles north of present-day Choteau.

Promoters who wanted to split up Montana's original Chouteau County proposed the name "Teton County" in the 1880s. The state Legislature created Teton County on March 1, 1893, and Choteau became its permanent county seat a year later. The tales of the county's creation are republished in this volume.

The tales that follow are mostly about the people, events and places in Choteau. The stories are true, or as true as the newspaper editors of the past 135 years believed to be true. Here and there the editors of the day left out information deemed too sensitive for their readers and those details are now lost to history.

My first book, "Tales from Montana's Rocky Mountain Front," captures stories from the 1870s to 1935, including the birth of Choteau, and my second book, "Tales from Montana's Teton County," captures stories from the 1920s to the 2000s.

Readers have enjoyed my historical vignettes, high-lights and old news tales published in the weekly Choteau Acantha newspaper since 1999. This third Tales volume continues my goal to introduce new readers to the local history of the region.

The stories in this volume are gleaned from the Choteau Acantha for the most part, although other newspaper accounts were used to research the tales. The newspaper began as the Dupuyer Acantha, published starting on Sept. 15, 1894. In early 1904 the Trescott brothers bought the Dupuyer Acantha's printing press and subscription list and moved the same to Choteau. They did not reset the volume numbers, but continued the newspaper as Vol. 10, No. 29, dated March 24, 1904. They renamed the newspaper, the Choteau Acantha, which has been continually published since that time under a succession of dedicated owners and publishers and their equally dedicated employees. The Acantha's history is republished in this volume.

For readers who want to read the original newspaper pages, visit the Montana Historical Society's website, www.montananewspapers.org. To read the current Choteau Acantha, visit the website, www.choteauacantha.com.

This book presents a collection of previously published stories highlighting local history, in mostly chronological order based on the year generally taken from story's subject matter. The dates under the chapter title are the dates the Acantha published them. Some text in this volume was edited or condensed from the original old news columns for clarity and to correct errors and conserve space as needed.

The Winter of 1884-85

November 21-28, 2018

The River Press in Fort Benton noted the first "beautiful" snow of the season in early October 1884, but the weather had already turned snowy closer to the mountains, some 80 miles to the west.

"Snowstorms have been raging in the mountains and along the foothills during the past week," reported a Choteau letter writer to the Sun River Sun newspaper on Sept. 13, "and we are forcibly reminded that now is the accepted time to lay in a winter's supply of firewood. By the way, you can get several new subscribers here if you will take firewood and rutabagas in payment."

In late October 1884, the River Press found something to worry about. "All of our local prophets, with a few of the outside precincts yet to hear from, are predicting a winter of unusual severity. Some of them say that during a season when berries are plenty, a cold winter is sure to follow. Of course, this must be so."

At the end of the article it dismissed the observation based on the "inexorable hand of science."

A post on Dec. 3 reflected the newspaper's optimism for a mild winter, at least in the vicinity of the foothills to the west of Fort Benton. "That portion of [Chouteau] county seems specially favored, as the snow does not stay long and the grass is most abundant. It is on the chinook belt, and from what we can learn, the good effects of that genial wind are felt to a greater extent than in almost any other portion of the territory."

In Choteau, however, the winter of 1884-85 would prove to be severe indeed.

In the tiny hamlet of Choteau, formerly called Old Agency, in November, the townsfolk learned of the first of several tragedies to come. Choteau's first newspaper was not published until Dec. 18, 1885, so the report comes from the River Press.

"Anton Warning, who left here on Nov. 13 for the mountains to get out some logs for his hay ranch, was found dead under a fallen tree near the head of the South Fork of the Muddy on Thanksgiving Day by Abel McKnight and Vitall Amarr of this place, who, alarmed by his long absence, had gone out to search for him.

"Warning's dog was sitting on the body with a note asking for help tied around his neck. Warning, evidently, had not succeeded in driving the dog away from him. The remains were brought to town and a coroner's jury empaneled, which found that deceased had come to his death accidentally. He was buried here yesterday."

The searchers found a written note, indicating Warning suffered an accident on Nov. 17. He must have died very shortly after writing it, the editor said, because his injuries were most severe.

"This memorandum is to certify that the undersigned met with an accident here as follows: On Monday night, being last night, I heard a crash, and by the time that I was fairly awake a fir tree came down on me, striking me about the abdomen and thighs, leaving my legs entirely powerless and also without any feeling, but I have severe pain in the abdomen, causing me to think that there is a rupture, and also a considerable pain in the breast, and especially in the spine, so that I am unable to rise to a sitting posture, or turn in my bed. I have to lie on my back constantly; I am constantly shaking, which I think is caused by the pain. If somebody don't come to the rescue pretty soon I expect I am done for this world.

"I sent a note tied in a faded blue silk handkerchief, but the chances are that I'll not be able to make him (the dog) leave camp.

"Hoping forgiveness of all the world, I conclude by signing myself, Anton Warning, Old Agency, Montana. Janesville, Wisconsin, the address of my sister Anna."

Warning, 24, was well liked by all who knew him, for his "quiet, unassuming manners, his industrious habits and his strict integrity."

As Choteau mourned the loss of one of its own, the temperatures plunged and stayed below zero, as recorded in Fort Benton, nearly every day in December. Winter had taken hold with a vengeance, and it would kill two more men from Choteau before spring.

A deep freeze descended on the region in December 1884, and on nearly every day the temperature never rose above zero degrees.

Fort Benton weather observer, B.O. Lenoir, noted the temperatures: -18 degrees on Dec. 15, -32 on Dec. 21, -47.5 on Dec. 22, -57.5 on Dec. 24 and -46 on Dec. 31. Fort Shaw noted -42 on Dec. 17.

"A report out of Wolf Creek dated Dec. 22 said the present severe cold weather and deep snow is making it almost impossible for the stage drivers to keep on time."

However, the news was that cattle on the open range were not suffering. "So far as reports from the outlying districts have been received, they are to the effect that no losses have been suffered by the stockmen by reason of the present 'cold snap.'

"The cattle were in unusually good condition, the ranges ditto and stock will suffer nothing further than a slight reduction in flesh," the River Press reported. "A single hoof has not been lost by reason of the cold weather, so far as is known up to this time. The sheepmen have fared equally well. They have been compelled, however, to 'rustle' pretty lively for the past two weeks and a decided inroad has been made on the haystacks. In many cases the snowplow has been used to good advantage, but there are about as many sheep in Montana as there were before the mercury commenced its dalliance with the degrees way below zero."

The paper noted that the amount of snow fallen so far in December was 11.4 inches and it snowed 13 days out of 24.

As the winter wore on, the River Press digressed from weather news to publish this report from Choteau.

"The enterprising town of Choteau, the metropolis of the Teton, is the headquarters of a number of cowboys. Some of them have recently gotten into trouble and are likely to feel the weight of the strong arm of the law. On the night of the 22nd, two days in advance of the holiday season, about a half a dozen of the boys concluded to begin their celebration, which was done by riddling the doors and windows of the Valley House with bullets from their trusty revolvers.

"Fortunately nobody was hurt, but several persons were badly scared. A warrant was sworn out before Judge Powers today and officers Caldwell and Forbes have gone to make the arrests. We trust they will be 'taken in' and punished severely. There is too much promiscuous shooting at Choteau for the good of the town and it ought to be stopped. The way to do it is to invoke the aid of the law as has been done in this case."

The Press noted a break in the weather when the temperature went from 39 below zero on Jan. 6, 1885, to 1 below zero on Jan. 7.

The Dupuyer correspondent on Jan. 13 said that on almost every morning from Dec. 14 to Dec. 20 the thermometer ranged from 20 below zero to 28 below zero, and from zero to 15 below during the warmer part of the day. On Dec. 23 it marked 40 below.

"Dan Sullivan on Birch Creek lost on account of the cold weather, 12 cows, several calves and a fine $700 stallion. His loss will reach nearly $2,000."

The Choteau correspondent on Jan. 17 said, "Robed in a mantle of beautiful snow, the scenery of our valley is pleasant to the eye, but, as regards temperature and outdoor comfort, very much on the shady side of romance. ...

"The thermometer has fallen as low as 46 below and with the exception of a chinook, which lasted 'too quick,' there has been a continuance of cold weather. Cattle are suffering, but having been in such good shape before the storm came on, they still are in a condition to rustle for some time.

"Our sheepmen, having supplied themselves with an ample quantity of hay and good corrals, can set the elements at defiance for some time to come. Let the wind blow high or low."

By Jan. 25, everyone thought the worst was over, but a "regular Dakota blizzard" nixed that.

2

Blizzard Kills Frank Farmer

Choteau cattle rancher Frank Farmer was having a good year with just one little snag.

He had taken up a ranch near the new town of Choteau, and supplemented his income as a Chouteau County road supervisor, responsible for "all that portion of the county from the lower Old Agency crossing north and west to the boundary line," a territory in the western fourth of the original Chouteau County before the state Legislature created Teton County in 1893. Old Agency was the name for Choteau's post office before the plat of the town of Choteau was recorded.

Farmer, about age 40, was a bachelor from Iowa who took a job as a Montana freighter in 1866. He settled in the Old Agency/Choteau area in 1876 and started working for stockowner Matthew Carroll. By 1882 he was raising his own herd.

In the days of the open range, Farmer, W.R. Ralston and E.D. Hastie were local cattle kings. The Oxley Ranch near Fort Macleod in Alberta had bought large herds from Montana cattlemen in the previous two years, and so the three men had no qualms about selling their herds to Oxley's paid agent J.R. Craig in July 1884.

Two weeks later — trouble — Craig's drafts to seal the deals were no good. The Sun River Sun newspaper said Craig had "repudiated the bargain," but the River Press in Fort Benton gave Craig the benefit of the doubt.

The Sun editor wrote, "We understand Craig gave Ralston a draft from I.G. Baker & Co. for $2,000, Hastie one for $1,000 and Farmer one for $1,000, to bind the bargain. The drafts were not honored when presented and it appears that the company had no credit with Baker & Co. We have been unable to learn why the bargain was broken. The action of Craig in the matter does not appear quite honest and the boys have a clear case of damages against him or his company, if the facts in the case are as we have learned."

A Press reporter, however, "made inquiries at Baker & Co. Thursday evening in regard to the matter when the subject was presented in a different light altogether.

"Before leaving this city Craig purchased 2,000 head of cattle from Baker & Co. and he telegraphed the fact to [Oxley Ranch Principal Manager] Lord Hill of England. He had instructions to buy 3,000 head and before receiving an answer from Hill he left for the Teton and made the purchases above mentioned. Meantime, a telegram came from Hill approving the first purchase and instructing Craig to stop buying.

"Without knowledge of these instructions, Craig bought the Teton herds and gave drafts on Baker & Co. for a small portion of each purchase price. When Ralston, Hastie and Farmer presented the drafts in this city, the circumstances were explained to them, and payment deferred until Hill could be heard from. Baker & Co. are confident that the purchase will be approved and that in due course of mail the money will be forthcoming. An answer is now daily expected.

"While it has been no doubt a disappointment to the gentlemen who sold their cattle, it is only justice to Craig to say that he acted in good faith and that a taint of dishonesty does not appear in the transaction," the Press wrote.

While the cattlemen waited for their money, the Sun

reported on Sept. 3, "The cattle lately purchased by Craig for the Oxley Ranch are still being held near the Teton River awaiting remittances from London to pay Hastie, Ralston and Farmer for the stock. Col. Higgins informs us that some few of the cattle are getting away every night, and that the whole band is losing flesh from this constant surveillance and restraint."

A Sept. 10 Press report said the cattle had been turned over to the purchaser and were "well on their way to that company's range in the Northwest Territory" with no word written about the deal's financial status.

After that, snowstorms and very cold weather set in, while the newspapers stayed mum about the soured deals. Then on Jan. 14, 1885, the Press reported that Col. J.J. Donnelly had commenced suit in the Chouteau County District Court on behalf of Ralston, Hastie and Farmer against the Oxley Ranch for $151,000.

The three men traveled by way of Sun River to Fort Benton, the county seat of Chouteau County, in the bitter cold winter of 1884-85.

Their lawsuit charged Oxley's agent Craig with contract default for nonpayment after he took possession of their herds. Craig argued miscommunication with the ranch officers in England, but he was unable to pay the purchase prices agreed upon, to Farmer, $12,000; to Ralston, $40,000; and to Hastie, $25,000.

The Press reported that the suit was for $151,000 but offered no further details. "This is for cattle purchased by the company from the plaintiffs last summer, only a small portion of the purchase money having been paid. This suit involves more money than any other ever commenced in the county and perhaps in the territory."

The ice on the lakes and ponds was about a foot thick, the temperature in December having been below zero nearly every day that month. Some reports said the cattle out on the open range were suffering; other reports said they were doing okay.

A letter writer named "Settler" from Marias Crossing told the Press on Jan. 21, "The recent storms have caused cattle to drift in large quantities, seeking protection from the inclement weather in the coulees and brush in this vicinity. There has been such an immense drift of them, that they have eaten the grass in the bottoms down as smooth as a floor, and are now ravaging the barnyards and haystacks; therefore causing a great deal of annoyance to settlers.

"We will also mention that they are crossing the Marias and Missouri rivers in crowding multitudes, and it will be well for stockmen who feel interested, to employ sufficient help to return them to their respective ranges, thereby saving a heavy expense in rounding up. Stockmen sitting around their fires at home do not seem to realize the condition their stock is in in this section of the country."

Then a "regular Dakota blizzard" blew in on Jan. 26. "It did not last long, but while it was with us it made things lively," the Press reported. "Old-timers say that it was the worst storm ever seen in this portion of Montana. It only lasted a few hours and passed away as quickly as it came."

By Jan. 28, the Press opined that the worst was over. The storm was gone, but the Choteau correspondent on Feb. 1 informed readers, "The events which have occurred in this section of the country during the past week, and which I propose relating now, have cast a gloom over our thriving little town."

He continued, "Although this is a beautiful Sabbath morning, our town seems nearly deserted by the male portion of the inhabitants, and what few are left may be seen in groups discussing the sad events which have lately occurred here, and which have resulted in one of our most worthy and esteemed citizens probably now lying in the cold embrace of death, solitary and alone on the broad prairie, and another highly esteemed citizen, who has often in all seasons of the year, ministered to the wants of the sick and afflicted, now an inmate of the government hospital at Fort Shaw, suffering from a broken and frozen limb and at the same time displaying a degree of courage and fortitude that is not often witnessed."

What followed was a story about Dr. Herbert Smith's accident. Smith and Ralston were traveling together south of Choteau when Smith's horse faltered, throwing the man. Ralston enlisted aid from town, but it was during the blizzard and Smith's health deteriorated before he was rescued. He never fully recovered and died in Choteau a few days later. A chapter in "Tales from Montana's Rocky Mountain Front" tells his life story.

On the same day that Ralston and the doctor left Choteau for Sun River, Farmer started for Dupuyer Creek. He reached Bynum's place, at the crossing of the Muddy, and after eating his dinner, saddled his horse and struck out for Dupuyer, after which nothing was heard of him.

A Choteau writer's news report dated Feb. 1 said, "A man reached here from that place [Dupuyer] last night and reported that Frank had not reached there. Messengers were immediately dispatched up and down the valley for assistance, and within one hour, 16 men, well mounted, started for Bynum's place, where they were to remain until daylight, when they would start and scout the country in search of poor Frank.

"At this time (3 p.m. Sunday) no news has been received from them. We can only hope for the best, but fear the worst. The chances of again seeing him with us, with his genial, smiling countenance, are indeed slim. I will here venture the assertion that there is no town or valley in Montana, or in the west, where you will find more noble, self-sacrificing men, always ready and willing to respond where the life of a fellow being is in danger, than in this quiet little town of Choteau and the valley surrounding it.

"True, reports have gone abroad that we are a lawless set around here, but believe nothing of the kind; come and see for yourselves and you will find that we have, in proportion to the population, as many whole-souled honorable men as can be found in any community."

The last paragraph was written at 8 p.m. "Ed. Dennis and Louis Morgan, who accompanied the party last night, have just arrived and report that they found the body of Frank Farmer near the road, lying on a snow drift, frozen stiff. His horse was feeding only a short distance from him; the saddle and bridle had been taken off and were lying near the body. Frank Farmer was one of God's noble men. Not an enemy had he that I ever heard of; and to think of his dying on the prairie so far from friends and relatives, with no kind hand to minister to his wants. What a sad warning for us all. 'In the midst of life we are in death.'"

His body was brought to Choteau the next day. With no coroner or justice of the peace in town at that time, the leading citizens viewed the body and agreed that Farmer was found lying on the prairie near the wagon road some four miles south of Dupuyer. They concluded that he met his death from exhaustion and exposure while traveling through deep snow during a severe blizzard on Jan. 26.

On Feb. 3, nearly all the inhabitants of Choteau and the Teton valley, besides a large number from the Muddy, Dupuyer and other outlying settlements, attended the funeral.

The Rev. W.J. Hunter of Sun River "preached a most affecting sermon, and it was a strange scene to witness the weather-beaten frontiersmen, hardy ranchmen and reckless cowboys overcome with grief at the sight of their old friend Frank lying cold in death's embrace. In the funeral procession, which was over a half-mile long, Frank's favorite horse, saddled and bridled, followed immediately after the hearse. The horse had stayed by Frank from the day of his death (Monday) until the Saturday following, when his body was found; and when the searching party approached, the faithful animal pricked up his ears, snorted and ran ahead of them up the snow drift to where Frank lay. Perhaps after the final grand roundup, Frank's horse will also be accorded a mansion."

In June fellow cattlemen Ralston and Hastie won their lawsuit and in August Farmer's estate won a judgment against the Oxley Ranch. The estate received the proceeds from the sale of 121 cows, 82 steers, 20 heifers, 68 calves, seven bulls and nine horses. The cattle with a brand sold for $36.50 per head and the horses averaged $49 each. Oxley's luckless agent Craig, who mistakenly contracted for the three men's cattle herds, was "absolutely dismissed" from the ranch's service in November.

After a public auction of Farmer's numerous items of personal property, the estate was closed in March 1886 on behalf of Farmer's relatives, while his two 160-acre, well-fenced ranches were sold in 1892.

3

Choteau House Comes Down

August 7, 2013

Choteau marked its 125th anniversary as a platted town in 2013, but its oldest commercial building, that in its heyday drew the dealmakers and movers and shakers of the community, was torn down early Sunday morning, Aug. 4, 2013.

Choteau House, more recently called the Choteau Bar & Steakhouse, located at 210 Main Ave. N., had not been open for business for more than five years and in recent months the interior was gutted in what had been expected to be a major remodeling project for a new restaurant, the Outlaw's Bar & Grill LLC, by owner-members Richard J. Rolandson of Choteau and Stephen L. Stenehjem of Watford City, North Dakota, who held the full-service liquor license, formerly under permit to the Choteau Steakhouse owner.

The 80-foot-wide, two-story building once contained a bar, a restaurant, a Laundromat and two upstairs apartments. The partnership, Montana Six Shooter LLP, purchased the building in August 2006, from Betty Hankins of Fort Benton.

Rolandson and Stenehjem were invited, but did not return Acantha queries, to discuss the future of the property. In an article for AAALiving.com in October 2007, Stenehjem is mentioned as having developed in summer 2006, the Outlaws Bar and Grill in Watford City, an upscale steakhouse open for lunch and dinner, decorated with wanted posters and an oxblood-red tin ceiling.

Teton County Sanitarian Corrine Rose once had a thick file on her many inspections of the Choteau Bar and Steakhouse, but after the business remained closed for five years, she decided to toss the file to make room for growing files on other businesses she inspected.

She said the new owners did not provide her with what is needed to obtain a food purveyor's license for a new business, namely, a floor plan, a menu and a list of equipment.

"It's a prime location," Rose said, explaining at the time that no other food-service establishments in Choteau had a full-service liquor license. Other restaurants in town had only beer and wine licenses. She said the American Legion Hall has a full service license, but it does not serve food on a daily basis.

"I had high hopes," Rose said, of the possible reopening of the restaurant.

In 2013 Kyle Harlan, a building inspector for the state Department of Labor and Industry in Great Falls, said he talked to Rolandson during the previous six or eight months, and expected to get a solid plan down on paper from him. Harlan inspected all non-residential structures of more than four units, and those used for transient guests.

He noted that the old building used to have a balcony, based on an old photo he saw. Indeed, pictures taken 100 years ago show the wood-frame building with a partial balcony.

Confederate soldier, miner and businessman George Richards built the Choteau Hotel and Bar in 1886, three years after Isaac Hazlett and Al Hamilton platted the town of Choteau.

In 1890, Richards sold the Choteau House to Englishman William Hodgskiss, who expanded the building in 1911 and who built a town hall that served as the county court house until the present one was built in 1906.

Hodgskiss sold the building to his son, William Jr., in 1923, and over the years, Choteau House had many owners, who each made their mark on the building, but who did not change the exterior very much.

In the early years, the local doctor had his office in the Choteau House, and many very sick people breathed their last breath while under his care there, including an old prospector, Fred Grant, in 1898, who was fatally injured by a reckless rider. The local newspaper reported the incident:

"As such an occurrence frequently happens in Choteau, no heed was paid the rider until he was in the front of Choteau House, when his horse was seen to slacken and falter near a hitching post. Immediately, the rider gave another war whoop, spurred his horse and was out of sight in the darkness before the bystanders had time to think. It was then discovered that an elderly and feeble man had been run over.

"Friends carried the limp and unconscious form into the Choteau House. The injured man was found to be Fred Grant, an old timer in Montana, who had been employed at the S.T. ranch for the past 30 days. A doctor was called and it was found that Grant was injured internally and within three hours after being hurt he died. Mr. Grant had just quit work at the S.T. ranch that afternoon and arrived in town about dusk. He was somewhat crippled up and while crossing the street was unable to get out of the way of the running horse, resulting in the accident."

Jerry Hamlin later confessed that he ran over Grant. He was riding a bronco without a bridle and was unable to control him. He was put on trial for manslaughter, but that's another story.

The late Ira Perkins told former Choteau House cook Elmer Schock, 70, that the bar witnessed many a deal to sell or buy cattle by a handshake or a hand-written draft,

Schock said in August 2013.

Schock recalled that he frequented the Choteau House before he could legally drink alcohol. He worked there in the early 1950s, when area ranchers had many hired hands, and a lot more people did their business in bars. He recalled the roughnecks who came to Choteau Steakhouse, when they were drilling for oil in the region.

"Choteau House drew people, especially when it had good cooks like Mary Jean Armstrong," Schock said. He remembers that Armstrong had candles on the tables. "It was busy then, a fancy eating place."

By 1965, the bar and restaurant were open 24 hours a day. Patrons at the bar had the option of eating breakfast after 2 a.m. if they were hungry. "When the bar closed, by then, you worked up an appetite," Schock said.

He remembered the "pipeliners" who arrived to build a pipeline near town. They came through and came to the bar for two or three weeks. "They were the worst characters. I was bartender then. One fight started at the bar then escalated at Rex's Market when one threw another man through Rex's window," Schock said.

Senior citizen Harry Agee remembered that all the big shots used the bar as a gathering place, including Tommy Larson who reportedly coined the phrase, Ditch Water, for a drink made with water and whiskey. "It was nothing to get meals at midnight," Agee said, but added that after many years the restaurant seemed to go "downhill."

Bert Guthrie said Choteau House was a gathering place for the older generation who were active in agriculture. "Lots of cattle and sheep bought and sold there," he said, adding that the prices would be negotiated over an evening and the sale consummated and delivery made shortly thereafter. Guthrie recalled traveling with his grandfather who would gather with the old timers in the afternoon at the Choteau House bar. Young Guthrie would drink a Coke and listen to the men talk of the old days.

By 1990, the Choteau Steak House and Casino had specials on its menu, including Elmer's homemade pizza on Wednesdays and $1 off all steaks Friday and Saturday nights.

Now that the old building is gone, Choteau residents have to wait to see what happens to this prime main street location.

4

Epidemic

Epidemic. The word is rarely used today, but in the early days of Choteau, the local newspaper editors had no qualms about using it to describe an illness that was being diagnosed more often than what would seem to be normal.

As early as December 1887, nearly half the residents in Choteau were "more or less afflicted with a sort of epidemic commonly called epizootic."

By January 1896, diphtheria was in the news. It was diagnosed in Mr. Richards' children and "nurses were employed to assist in taking care of the sick and the house was quarantined until all danger from spreading the malady should pass." The Montanian newspaper published the cure: Take sulphur, borax and salt petre in equal parts, ground fine. Take a goose quill filled with the mixture and touch the white spots when they appear, blowing the powder into the mouth. Apply three or four times a day."

Two years later, measles was epidemic in Choteau, and "all over the berg cases indicating febrile symptoms are making their appearance day by day." Editor S.M. Corson added reassuring words after the alarming ones, "The cases mentioned heretofore are now convalescing and will soon be able to appear upon the streets in their usually hilarious and gleeful style as heretofore. No serious results from this epidemic have as yet been reported."

Not to be left out, mumps made an appearance in the news columns in May 1900: "Miss Addie Penry closed her school in Belleview district two weeks ago on account of an epidemic of the mumps, the teacher as well as all the pupils being affected." In the same issue the City Drug Store advertised "White Pine Expectorant, a valuable combination for croup and colds."

Sometimes, though, the situation was scary. In January 1905, Miss Marguerite Jones, a teacher in the Choteau public schools, was reported sick with smallpox at the home of A.M. Kennedy where she had been boarding since her return to town from a holiday vacation at Billings, where smallpox was "fiercely raging."

Authorities "vigorously enforced" the quarantine regulations. The Board of Health instructed the sheriff to kill all cats and dogs running at large after due notice of 24 hours to keep such cats and dogs in close confinement, closed all public buildings in Choteau for a day, while they were thoroughly fumigated; and ordered that all people who attended the Masonic ball on Jan. 20, 1905, and all children in town be quarantined at their homes for five days, among other orders.

Although only Miss Jones and four other people got sick, the scare prompted the county to build a new "pest house" and also a "detention hospital" at the poor farm outside of town.

The Choteau Acantha noted: "The amount of disinfectants used in Choteau has permeated the earth and a part of the sky in the vicinity of the town. We make this observation to allay any feelings of alarm that might arise in the minds of residents in neighboring towns on account of a flock of wild geese having passed over our city last evening. We guarantee the geese free from the germs of smallpox."

— 5 —

The County Jail

April 18, and 25, 2018

Local lore pegs the first jail in Choteau to be that squat squarish building, circa 1893, that sits just west of the Teton County Law Enforcement Center, but a search of the old news places the first official jail back in September 1887.

Choteau was a fledgling four-year-old town back then, complete with all sorts of characters including horse thieves. It was the embarrassing escape of one, James Marshall, that prompted the townsfolk to petition the Chouteau County commissioners for help in building a jail.

The River Press in Fort Benton chronicled the incident in December 1886. "About Dec. 2 or 3 Stock Inspector Billy Watts arrested a man named Marshall at Choteau, who was accused of horse stealing. (Another account says the Mounted Police apprehended Marshall the first time.)

"Inspector Watts placed the prisoner in charge of Charley Munn to guard while he went to Helena to secure witnesses against him. A few nights afterwards, while Munn had his prisoner in a closed room under a guard, a gentleman opened the door and stepped inside, not knowing the state of affairs. Seizing the opportunity, the prisoner quickly stepped out of the door onto the street and fled. The gentleman who came in naturally closed the door after him all unconscious of what had happened.

"Munn sprang to the door and out into the darkness; he could see nothing, but listening could hear the prisoner running and fired one or two shots after him without

22

effect. Munn secured assistance and tried to find his man that night but was unsuccessful.

"Subsequently it was ascertained that Marshall went up to Sam Mitchell's place about two miles above Choteau and stole a horse, saddle and bridle from the stable. He was next heard of at Birch Creek, 40 odd miles north of Choteau, where he again entered a stable and stole a horse from John Wren who happened to be there with his team.

"The horse stolen from Mitchell's was found on the prairie nearby next morning much jaded. Maj. Baldwin at the Blackfoot Agency, being informed of what had happened, immediately sent three of his trusted mounted Indian police, with fresh horses on Marshall's trail, and in all probability they will capture him.

"Munn and pursuing party were only five hours behind at the agency. A short distance north of the agency a cow was found lately killed, from which but a few pounds of meat had been taken. This was supposed to have been done by Marshall. The horse stolen from [Mitchell] had been driven all the day previous and was in no condition to travel."

The River Press opined, "The horse thief, who made his escape at Choteau, as related in another column, was of rather an accommodating turn. While Stock Inspector Watts was at Helena hunting evidence against him, he very generously stole two more horses, so there couldn't be any doubt about it. Nothing like being accommodating."

There's no news of Marshall being found, and the Choteau Calumet editor on Dec. 17, wrote, "The escape of Marshall, the horse-thief, furnishes more evidence of the importance of having a jail at Choteau. As a matter of economy it should interest the county commissioners at once, and as a matter of safety to life and property, it concerns every law-abiding citizen of the community. If a jail cannot be secured in any other way, it would pay to build it by subscription."

In March 1887, the Calumet reported that the citizens of Choteau "have petitioned the Board of County Commissioners to erect a jail, or lock-up, in this town as early as convenient. We have a number of competent builders here who would contract to do the work in a substantial and satisfactory manner, and as the commissioners were fully empowered by the late Legislature to build jails wherever required, there appears to be no good reason why we should not have one at once."

Chouteau County Commissioners W.G. Conrad and Chas. Wegner heard the petition on April 6, 1887, and they directed the clerk to request the signers to furnish an estimate of the size and cost of the jail and to include purchasing a lot for the proposed jail.

That took until July, when the commissioners noted that they were willing to accept the submitted estimate for the Choteau jail, but they objected to the fence that was part of the plan, so it bounced back to the townsfolk.

The River Press was the county newspaper of record for Chouteau County before Teton County was formed in March 1893. But Choteau was blessed with a newspaper all its own and on Sept. 3, 1887, the Calumet reported, "James Gibson and John Jackson Jr. returned from jury duty at Benton on Wednesday. Mr. Gibson states that it was understood at Benton that the commissioners, before they adjourned, provided for the long promised bridge across the Teton and the jail at Choteau."

The following week the Calumet told readers, "The Board of County Commissioners appropriated the munificent sum of $500 to purchase ground and build a jail at Choteau. After the lot is bought, there will be about money enough left to chalk out a jail." (In fact, inflation pegs $500 in the year 1887 equal in purchasing power to $12,674.14

in 2018.)

It's not clear where the jail was built, but on Sept. 8 Commissioners R.S. Ford and Chas. Wegner authorized Justice of the Peace Ed. C. Garrett and Deputy Sheriff H.W. Kelly to build it. Garrett was the master of ceremonies when the cornerstone was laid. "The material is on the ground and the edifice will be completed within 30 days," the Calumet said.

On Dec. 8, 1887, the commissioners examined the deed and bills for the jail construction and approved the same, without comment that the cost was actually $527.65. O.G. Cooper sold the county a town lot for $50. The other payments were to: N.A. McDonald, $162; Jacob Schmidt, $214.63; J. Hirshberg & Co., $52.85; Silverman & Cohen, $9.95; P.N. Knowles, $25; B. Racine, $5; and Garrett, $8.

Things appear to have quieted down after that, with no one reported as having been arrested and locked up until June 23, 1888.

"Eliza Merchant, daughter of the late Fred Merchant, was arrested and locked up on Friday night last by Deputy Sheriff Kelly. Saturday morning the frail Eliza was arraigned in the justice court charged with disorderly conduct, but in consideration of her extreme youth, the girl is hardly more than 15 years of age, and tearful promises of immediate and radical reform, his honor Judge Garrett dismissed her with a few words of kindly advice."

Merchant had grown up in Fort Benton, but was in Choteau when her father, Fred, died in a Helena jail of alcoholism in September 1887. Fred had been a barkeeper born in England and Eliza's mother, Sallie, was a black woman born in Virginia.

Another Calumet column reported: "The tomb-like silence which usually pervades the hall of justice in law-abiding Choteau was enlivened this week by a serious case of jail breaking.

"On Friday evening Eliza Merchant was locked up. An hour or so later two men were discovered by Sheriff Kelly apparently trying to break into the jail. The sheriff knocked one of the men down and sent a bullet after the other, who ran away, but was subsequently arrested.

"The prisoners, who proved to be John McCue and Frank Moyers, were locked up for the night and brought before Judge Garrett for examination early the following morning. McCue was bound over in the sum of $500 to await the action of the grand jury, but Moyers, who proved that he was not trying to open the jail, was ordered to give bonds to the amount of $500 to appear as witness against McCue. As the men could not furnish bonds, they were sent to Benton.

"Probably McCue had little notion of the serious nature of his attempt to visit Miss Merchant by breaking open the jail door, and while the law may not recognize a difference between his object and an effort to rescue a condemned criminal, it is a case we think, in which a large degree of charity might be safely exercised."

The court took its time, but eventually in November 1888s McCue was indicted for jail breaking. Found guilty, he was sentenced to 18 months in the penitentiary and to pay a fine of $100 for breaking into jail.

Merchant and McCue were never in the news again, but the first Choteau jail would be mentioned until 1894 when the new jail was ready for occupancy.

6

Thanksgiving 1891

November 25, 2015

By a coincidence of the calendar, Thanksgiving Day 2015 fell on Nov. 26, something that happens every few years, including the year 1891.

On Dec. 4, 1891, Choteau Montanian Editor S.M. Corson wrote, "Nov. 26 was a day of thanksgiving in Choteau in every sense of the word. The people had much to be thankful for and that they appreciated it was apparent on every face.

"Family gatherings around many a groaning table was the order of the day rather than the exception. Everyone was happy and thankful for so great a boon.

"In the evening the Knights of Pythias gave a ball in Choteau Hall on Main Street, which was largely attended by 58 gay cavaliers and their ladies. The ball was a decided success socially and, we are reliably informed, netted the association a small profit.

"During the day, several horse races took place on the bench east of town, but the fierce wind which blew at times during the day prevented many from attending them. In fact, none but those directly interested in them and the horses ventured out to see the performance.

"People generally gave themselves up to feasting and thanksgiving," Corson said.

It wasn't the first time a fraternal organization or group hosted a Thanksgiving event in Choteau.

The first published mention of a Thanksgiving ball in

Choteau was on Nov. 18, 1885, in the Fort Benton River Press. The Teton Lodge No. 18, Independent Order of Odd Fellows, hosted a Thanksgiving ball, with the organizers cited as being "the most prominent and influential men in that section." The editor added, "A good time may be expected as the Choteau people never do anything by halves."

Fort Benton men Sam Kohlberg and Jere Sullivan instituted the new Knights of Pythias Lodge in Choteau a month later, and its members organized a Christmas ball.

The Choteau Calumet newspaper wrote a year later, "The Chevalier Lodge No. 12, K. of P., will give their annual ball on the 28th instant, and from the preparations in progress it is safe to say that it will be an unusually fine affair.

"These society balls are always a success at Choteau. As mentioned in a late issue, the Thanksgiving ball of Teton Lodge No. 18, IOOF, was the best attended and in every other respect the most satisfactory entertainment of the kind that has ever been held in the county."

By 1887, the Ladies Church Organization was hosting a Thanksgiving supper and the Choteau Social Club did the same the following year, which leads us back to 1891. Tickets for the Knights of Pythias's Thanksgiving ball on Nov. 26 were $3 each and that included "supper, good music and a general good time assured."

Corson included Pres. Benjamin Harrison's Thanksgiving proclamation in the Nov. 20 issue. It said in part, "I appoint the 26th day of November to be a day of joyful thanksgiving to God for the bounties of His providence, for the peace in which we are permitted to enjoy them, and for the preservation of those institutions of civil and religious liberty which he gave our fathers wisdom to devise and establish and courage to preserve. Among the appropriate observances of the day are rest from toil, worship in public congregation, renewal of family ties about our American firesides and thoughtful helpfulness toward those who suffer a lack of body or of spirit."

Montana Gov. Joseph K. Toole's proclamation followed. He wrote, "The second year of statehood has filled the full measure of prophecy. From every source comes the glad news of prosperity and contentment. Every business has increased with the years. Mines and mills are in full blast. Stock and range are prepared to challenge the winter. Agriculture, made certain of maturity and prolific of yield by irrigation, is opening a new field for capital and labor.

"Our people are generally employed and government is felt, if at all, most in its benefits and least in its restraints. These are ample to demand our recognition of divine favor and to call for a day of thanksgiving and prayer. I appoint as such Nov. 26, 1891.

"On that day let business be suspended and give to the great heart of humanity a chance to do good."

7

Dr. Simeon Drake
Builds a Hospital

April 6, 13, 20, 27, May 4, 11, 18, 2016

Montanian editor Shuler M. Corson expressed his frustration on Dec. 25, 1891, when he wrote, "Never before were the necessities for a hospital at this place so painfully felt as today. Three men lie wounded almost to death and no place to take them to."

In Choteau's pioneer days starting in the 1880s, people who were badly injured or who needed an operation sought help at the military hospital in Fort Shaw, or before Teton County was created in 1893, sought assistance at county facilities in Fort Benton.

And then the perfect storm of emergencies happened.

"On Wednesday just after dinner, seven sticks of giant powder which were thawing on the stove at Tom McGovern's ditch camp, about two miles south of town, exploded and severely injured Albert Bouscaren and Mike Kelly.

"Kelly was bending over the stove handling the powder when it exploded. His right leg was broken above the ankle and his face and body burned and cut by the pieces of stove, which filled the air. His clothing was set on fire and, but for the arrival of those working on the ditch nearby, he would have burned to death.

"Young Bouscaren, a son of engineer Julius Bouscaren and who was timekeeper on the works, was just entering the tent when the explosion occurred. He was struck in many places on the body by flying bits of stove and badly burned. His left leg was struck at the shoe top, the bone broken and the flesh torn away. How either of them escaped being torn to atoms is a miracle.

"Aleck Monkman, who had but a moment before left the tent, was the first to reach it after the explosion. He says Bouscaren was crawling out from the debris on his hands and knees but did not seem to be much hurt. Kelly was yet inside and Bouscaren said that he was on fire and burning up. A peep inside the shattered tent disclosed the unfortunate old man wrapped in flames and writhing with pain upon the ground. Assistance quickly arrived and the burning clothes removed.

"Monkman then jumped on a horse and came to town after Dr. Wamsley, who proceeded at once to the scene of the accident. After caring for them the best he could, the wounded men were brought to town, their wounds dressed and broken bones set. This morning Dr. Wamsley informs us that both men are doing well, though it's a little too soon to determine the full extent of their injuries," Corson wrote on Dec. 25, 1891.

On the same page, Corson told the story of Gus Momberg's plight.

"As though not sufficient unto the day were the evils thereof, late Wednesday night Wm. Wagner made an assault upon the person of Gus Momberg, shooting him in the hip with a revolver. The particulars are as follows:

"Wagner came to Momberg's house, about 12 miles northwest of Choteau, intending to remain overnight. At bedtime he was shown to a bed upstairs but he soon came down, saying he would not sleep there.

"He quarreled with his host about the accommodations given him. In reply to a query as to what he was going to do about it, he replied by drawing his revolver and firing at

Momberg, the ball entering near the point of the hip. The wounded man fell and Wagner attempted to fire again when Mrs. Momberg, who had retired for the night, sprang between them and pushed the murderer out the door, which she locked.

"Fastening up the house securely, she ran to neighbors, half a mile distant, and gave the alarm. A messenger was dispatched for the doctor and officer, both of whom arrived in due time. On the wife's return home she found her husband lying on the floor with a gun by his side ready for attack. The wounded man had crawled to where his gun was kept and was ready for self-defense. Dr. Wamsley and officer Adlam soon arrived and the wounded man cared for and later Wagner was arrested at a neighbor's, brought to town and lodged in jail where he now is awaiting an exam before Justice Dunlap.

"Last evening the wounded man was brought to Choteau and is now at his brother-in-law's, Jas. Armstrong, under the care of Dr. Wamsley. This morning he reported the wound as serious, though not necessarily fatal, the ball having coursed outside instead of inside, as was at first supposed, and lodging in the fleshy part of the upper part of the thigh. The wound is a particularly painful one."

Bouscaren and Kelly slowly recovered from their injuries, although they had to heal in private homes because no hospital existed in Choteau in December 1891.

Bouscaren's father, Julius, a well-known civil engineer, had been a resident of Choteau since at least 1890.

He was an incorporator of the Montana Northern Railroad Co., that wanted to build a line from Great Falls through Choteau and Dupuyer to reach the Canadian border, but that specific route was never built.

Albert Bouscaren and his brother, Willie, arrived in Choteau in July 1891, and their dad immediately got Al a job on a ditch project he was engineering. On a frigid day during the week before Christmas 1891, Al and Kelly nearly died in the explosion. In February, young Bouscaren was able to sit up, the news report said.

According to the Montanian newspaper, the contractor in charge of the ditch camp, Tom McGovern, "did a handsome thing for the two unfortunate men who were blown up by giant powder at his ditch camp last week. He offered up a horse at a raffle for $200 and donated the proceeds for their benefit. One hundred chances were taken at $2 each. Johnnie Mitchell won the horse."

By March Al had healed under the skilled care of Dr. Wamsley, but Al's father decided to quit Choteau and head for New Orleans. He closed his office and sought a "new field of operations," the news report said.

Kelly, on the other hand, appears to have made slow progress. He was walking on crutches in February, but on April 22, 1892, the Montanian reported, "he left on Thursday for Fort Benton, where he will go into the county hospital for awhile."

Nearly two years passed, and in that time Teton County was established and the county commissioners established a "poor fund" and a "poor farm."

Kelly's obituary, a tribute of sorts, appeared in the May 18, 1894, newspaper. It said Michael "Kelly" Brennan, was a native of Ireland. He was a Civil War veteran and served for 10 or 15 years after that. "Mike was as tough, physically, as a hickory withe, and had passed safely through many hardships and hairbreadth 'scapes. The last of these was when a couple of years ago he was blown up by giant powder and disfigured.

"Mike was his only and worst enemy. His only vice was whiskey. In all else he was a good man and a patriot, but, like many who served their country, he went unrewarded and finally died at the poor farm, but not until death had marked him for his own did he allow himself to become a county charge. Rest easy, Mike."

Meanwhile, the third man who had been wounded, Gus Momberg, completely recovered. He had been shot on Dec. 24, 1891, at his home by an unwelcome guest, William Wagner.

Deputy George Adlam arrested Wagner at a neighbor' house. Adlam told the newspaper, "Wagner expresses great grief over the shooting and cannot imagine why he done it, as he had nothing in the world against him. He was drunk at the time and knew not what he was doing. But the law recognizes no such excuses and Wagner says he knows it." Wagner was convicted in March and sentenced to three years' imprisonment.

Momberg recovered at a relative's house in Choteau and in February returned to his ranch. He and his large family moved to the Blackfeet Reservation; his wife was one-half Piegan Indian. He died in December 1906 from cancer and was buried in Browning.

Which brings us to the formation of the first hospital in Choteau. Dr. Simeon H. Drake of Butte announced his intention to relocate to Choteau in the Oct. 7, 1892, Montanian. He opened offices upstairs in the Valley Hotel, where the former Meeting Grounds eatery was located until a few years ago. His practice grew at the same time he was appointed as the first coroner of the newly-formed Teton County.

He also secured the contract for furnishing medicines and medical treatment to the county poor for $800 per annum and 50 cents mileage outside of 10 miles from town, and in May he bought the stock of drugs and fixtures of W.B. Henry, reopened Henry's drugstore one day a week and invited his grown son, Clarence, to take charge of it two years later.

The physician and surgeon began treating patients in October 1892 and the local newspaper made mentions of Drake's recovering patients every so often. His practice expanded in March 1893 into a "nicely located" suite of rooms above the Bank of Choteau, where the benefit was "having a private consultation room, away from prying eyes and ears."

The injuries that the townsfolk suffered were often written about in gruesome detail such as the man "who had fallen off a wool wagon near Priest's Butte, and had his legs broken by the wheels passing over his thighs."

A month later, readers learned, "Dr. Drake's hospital patients are both doing well. The one whose leg was crushed some two weeks since near Priest's Butte will be out on crutches in a few days."

It is unclear where Drake housed his patients at that time, but readers learned that the Drake family occupied Mrs. Nat Collins's residence, pending the construction of one of their own.

Drake's success was assured when encouraging reports like this one were published.

"William Hodgskiss met with a painful accident while out gunning with a party of friends Wednesday evening. It appears that the party was in the fields up the Teton and had scattered out in quest of chickens. Soon a bird was flushed and Casey fired at the low-flying bird just as it got in line with Mr. Hodgskiss, who endeavored to get out of the way by stooping, but not low enough.

"Several of the shot penetrated the socket of his left eye and side of the nose, and more struck him in the hand and leg. The wounded man was brought to town and Dr. Drake summoned, who, after a careful examination, pronounced the eye safe and uninjured except what might result from inflammation. Yesterday the doctor reported that he did not think any of the shot had remained in the wounds, the glancing direction having carried them out after breaking the flesh. The wound is a most painful one but will not result seriously."

All through 1894, Dr. Drake worked to find better locations for his home and his businesses, but he also had time to run unsuccessfully for a two-year term as coroner on the Republican ticket. His appointment as the first coroner expired in December 1894.

No matter, Drake was busy designing his hospital. In March 1895 the Montanian newspaper reported, "Work was begun on Dr. Drake's hospital building Monday morning, and already the greater part of the walls of the main building are up. The erection of a good hospital here will be a great boon to many a sufferer, as there is no place nearer than Great Falls where a patient can be treated."

On March 22, 1895, the Montanian announced, "The Teton County Sanitarium. The building for this institution is now under roof and will be completed in two weeks, if the weather gets warm enough to allow the plastering to be done. The present building consists of four dormitories, a large general room and a double sitting and a bedroom connected by an archway.

"The whole is arranged in a manner to secure privacy and quiet for the sick, the large general room furnishing a comfortable and pleasant resort for convalescents and those not sick enough to be confined to their rooms.

"An experienced nurse will be employed and care and attendance equal to any hospital in the West will be furnished at the most reasonable rates.

"The plan of the institution contemplates a bath house supplied with medicated baths, such as sulfur, electric, etc. There will also be a Turkish bath.

"An institution of this kind is greatly needed in this locality, where there are so many men without homes and for whom it has been, heretofore, very difficult to provide suitable accommodations in case of sickness or accident. Especial arrangements have been made for receiving and caring for ladies who cannot on account of distance from medical aid or any other cause, be conveniently attended at their own homes.

"Temporary arrangements have been made for receiving patients now, caring for them until the sanitarium is completed. Address for terms and information. S.H. Drake. M.D."

By April 1895, Drake was well established in his public as well as his private medical practice, having built a small hospital on Choteau Avenue, which is now First Street Northwest.

The only blemish on his esteemed record came in August 1895 when he was accused by some folks in Dupuyer and by Dupuyer Acantha publisher C.E. Trescott of negligence in treating George Legacy, an Albertan down on his luck who asked for a drink in Hunter's saloon one day. The controversy continued through the trial in October of accused shooter Jack Tenney, also known as John Tenny.

The story begins a bit earlier, in July 1895 when "last evening Tenney was set upon by two persons and was severely pounded over the head with rocks and clubs and in some manner had his right leg broken at the ankle — probably by being struck with a club while insensible and was left by them for dead."

Tenney later identified Ed Shea as one of the assailants, and in a month's time a jury in Justice Beaupre's court found Shea guilty of assault and battery. The jury fixed the penalty at 30 days in the county jail and fined Shea $25 and costs.

That Tenney himself and others may not have thought justice had been served was shown in the Acantha's statement, "In this scrap Shea only half killed his man. It would be interesting to know if the same jury would have given him only 60 days and $50 if he had made a good job of it."

Tenney soon got around on crutches as his body healed, but some speculated later that his mind did not.

"On Sunday evening, the 28th of July, George Legacy, a Frenchman who has been in this vicinity for a few weeks, stepped into Hunter's saloon and asked Jack Tenney, who was temporarily behind the bar, for a drink, which was refused. The men then entered into a conversation, but it was held in such a low tone that no part of the conversation was heard by persons in the saloon at the time, until Legacy was again heard to ask for a drink. Tenney reached under the bar, but instead of bringing to view the desired bottle, produced a 45-Colt's six shooter, and, with the remark to 'take that you s— of a b— and see how you like it,' shot Legacy down in cold blood.

"As nearly as can be learned at the present time there had been no quarrel between these men, and there was apparently no cause for the shooting, but the impression is gaining ground that there is existing between them some old grudge. Nothing definite is known, however, as both parties have refused to make any statements," the Acantha said.

The competing newspaper, the Montanian, also wrote about the incident as told by a witness. "Tenney made no effort to escape and stood like one dazed with the smoking weapon in his hand. Sam Potter said, 'What are you doing, Tenney?' but he made no answer and offered no resistance when Potter took the revolver from him."

In a possible explanation, the Montanian said, "Legacy was from Alberta, Northwest Territories, near Mcleod, where he is said to have a ranch and possibly some stock. Some letters were found on his person but there was no money, he having been broke for some time and hunting work. He was in Choteau some weeks ago and from here went out shearing and later got stranded in Dupuyer, where he met his death at Jack Tenney's hands. ... Tenney did not want Shea arrested, claiming that he (Tenney) would take care of him. The other man, whose name we do not remember, escaped at the time, but on Sunday he was in town, and it is presumed that when Tenney fixed his gun he was preparing for his reception as he had threatened to shoot him on sight."

Legacy was brought to Mrs. Dean's hotel nearby in Dupuyer and a few days later he died. That is where Dr. Drake's reputation came into play.

"Dr. Drake, the county physician, arrived there about 1 o'clock yesterday afternoon, stopping with Dr. Gillette for two hours, or more, until after the man was dead. Great indignation against the doctor was felt by the people there for his neglect to attend the wounded man at the earliest possible moment after his arrival at Dupuyer."

Legacy was dead, Tenney was in jail, and county physician Drake, was in the hot seat accused of having neglected to treat Legacy in the hours before he died of a gunshot wound.

Dr. Drake had a prosperous career in Choteau, as the county physician and in his private practice, even to the point of building the county's first hospital, but Legacy's death in Dupuyer challenged his credentials for a time, especially because the editor of the Dupuyer Acantha was out to "roast" him over the incident.

On July 28, 1895, Tenney shot Legacy through the right breast with a 45-caliber Colt revolver. Bystanders brought Legacy to Mrs. Dean's hotel where Dr. Henry Gillette examined him and treated his pain with opiates.

Gillette and his wife had been residents of Dupuyer since 1884, when he resigned as the Blackfeet Agency physician. He chose to be a rancher, not a regular licensed practicing doctor, but he was willing and ready at any time to assist any of his neighbors who were sick or injured, even though he was taking great chances when he prescribed for a sick person, the rival newspaper, the Choteau Montanian, said.

The rumors started after Legacy died. "Dr. Drake, the county physician, arrived there about 1 o'clock yesterday afternoon, [Aug. 1] stopping with Dr. Gillette for two hours, or more, until after the man was dead. Great indignation against the doctor was felt by the people there for his neglect to attend the wounded man at the earliest possible moment after his arrival at Dupuyer," Montanian publisher S.M. Corson said.

Dupuyer Acantha publisher Trescott fueled the flames with this over-the-top diatribe, having jumped to what would turn out to be numerous false conclusions: "May the God of heaven have mercy on the sick and infirm poor of Teton County as long as S.H. Drake of Choteau is the county physician. For cold-blooded, barbarous treatment to persons under his care he stands without a peer.

"Last Sunday afternoon poor George Legacy was shot, and word was sent to the county seat to the county physician. Monday came and he failed to put in his appearance. That night Dr. Wamsley of Choteau, who was out here on private business, was called in to see the man, but could do nothing for him, as he had no medicine or surgical instruments with him. On his return to Choteau, however, he put up medicine and sent it out, and caused word to be sent to the county physician that his services were needed at Dupuyer.

"Tuesday passed and no physician. Word was again sent to Choteau. Wednesday passed, but no physician was in sight, and poor Legacy was suffering the tortures of the damned. Thursday, about noon, four days after the shooting, the county physician arrived, accompanied by the undersheriff. On his way here Drake was repeatedly asked to urge his team along and told that the man was probably dying.

"It is the Acantha's opinion that a physician with a heart as large as a chicken's, would call at the bedside of a wounded man as soon as he arrived in town, even if he was three or four days in getting there. But what did Drake do? Immediately on arriving in town he went to the house of a friend and stayed there fully two hours and a half! He must have had a heart of stone!

"Word was sent over to Drake while at his friend's house that poor Legacy was sinking, and the messenger was informed that he would 'be over in awhile.' In the meantime Legacy had died. And this is a man who has the contract for attending the sick and infirm poor of Teton County!

"With full knowledge of the fact that Legacy was about to breathe his last, he calmly sat down to a table and spent two hours in discussing the various delicacies spread before him. No thought had he then of the poor unfortunate who was about to be ushered into the great beyond.

"While it is undoubtedly true that this wound in the person of Legacy was necessarily fatal, common humanity demands that a physician who has been sent for, should call as soon as possible and relieve, as far as he is able, the sufferings of the wounded man.

"It is one of the most fortunate things in the world that Undersheriff Cramer was with Drake today. The citizens of Dupuyer are justly indignant at the shameful neglect he has shown in this case. Strong talk of a coat of tar and feathers for him were heard on every corner," Trescott concluded.

The uproar over accusations that Drake had been negligent in his official duties elicited responses that filled an entire page of the Aug. 9, 1895, Montanian.The Montanian published statements by Drake, Gillette, Cramer and County Attorney James Sulgrove. Drake's statement began, "I do this for the benefit of the general public as I feel assured that any person who knows me will need no explanation.

"In the first place, the man was not a county charge and had no right to the county physician as such, which is proved by the fact that the county commissioner who was in Dupuyer when the shooting occurred did not notify the county physician that his services were needed, either at that time or at any subsequent period.

"I was never notified by anyone, whether public or private, at any time whatsoever that my services were desired, either as county or private physician, but I was reliably informed not only that Legacy was being cared for by Dr. Gillette, but that a citizen of Dupuyer had come to Choteau and procured medicine for him. Some of which I saw when visiting Legacy and which the nurse assured me he had been giving according to directions. ...

"The very nature of Legacy's wound prevented any certain diagnosis to be made, as the outer marks might, or might not be, an index of the amount of internal injury, and as Legacy during all his illness suffered very little pain, all were hopeful of a favorable result.

"On Tuesday morning, a county commissioner found Legacy sitting on the side of the bed smoking a cigar, and saying he would be herding sheep in a week or two. Then on Wednesday, I heard he was worse, and on Thursday I decided to go to Dupuyer, as it had been suggested to me by the county attorney that he would like to have my testimony in regard to the wound in case Legacy should die and Tenney be tried for murder."

Drake described how Cramer, who was delayed because his horses had gotten out of the pasture, came for him, the long buggy ride — three hours and 50 minutes — and how he met with Gillette first, as medical ethics prescribed.

Gillette told him that he feared Legacy was fatally hurt, Drake said, but he had just seen him an hour before, and he did not expect the man to die that day or for a week. Gillette offered Drake some lunch, which took awhile to prepare, because the lunch hour had long past.

Drake continued, "But in one hour and 10 minutes after my arrival, I was at Legacy's bedside, he having died from a sudden effusion of a large quantity of blood into his chest cavity," whereas before, the autopsy supported, it apparently only had been gradually oozing from the injured lung.

Drake said, "Had I known, I should not have lost a moment, but from Dr. Gillette, I knew that nothing could have been done."

The other narrators backed up Drake's story, which refuted Trescott's allegations made the previous week.

The sequence of events became important at Tenney's trial in October 1895 when his court-appointed defense attorneys, J.E. Erickson and J.G. Bair, argued that Tenney did not commit murder. They said Legacy died, not from the wound, but from lack of proper medical attendance, and besides, Tenney was not in a rational state of mind at the time, because he had received injuries about the head and body a few weeks prior in July.

Montanian publisher Corson recapped the trial almost verbatim in the Oct. 4 edition, including the judge's jury instruction. "Judge Pomeroy knocked the alleged lack of medical treatment theory out by instructing them that had no medical attention whatever been given the wound and the man had died, you cannot find in that a cause for his death.

The wound must be considered the cause of death except where malpractice sufficient to cause death is proved." As the defense did not argue malpractice, the jurors were compelled to conclude that Legacy died from the effects of the wound, Corson wrote.

Deliberating for about an hour and a half, the jury returned a verdict of guilty in the second degree and fixed the penalty as imprisonment for life, reportedly reached on second ballot, the first having stood six for second degree, five for first and one for manslaughter, Corson wrote.

Acting Gov. Miles paroled Tenney, also known as John Tenny, on May 15, 1908, after Tenney was refused parole in 1903. Drake was no longer alive by then.

With the verdict of guilty in the Tenney murder trial in October 1895, county physician Simeon Drake, M.D., was vindicated in a controversy over medical care to the victim.

By December Dr. Drake had won renewal of the county poor contract, but the news had only a few reports referencing his small hospital during the following years. He erected a building to house his drugstore business, and he put on an addition for an ice cream and reading room with a marble soda fountain.

The following August he was treating diphtheria patients, but that was in tents about 200 feet apart, apparently set up east of town.

In April 1897, he treated the county's most famous celebrity, Baron Maximilian von Grotthuss in the man's last illness. A native of Russia, Grotthuss was banished by the Czar for political reasons, coming to New York City, where he met the sheep men, the Clark brothers, and with them came to Choteau.

In December 1898 the Montanian reported, "Dr. Drake has just fitted up two wards in his residence to be used for hospital purposes and is now prepared to receive patients to where they will have the attention of experienced nurses and the best of care as well as medical attendance." There was no word as to what he did with the old hospital building.

Then in May 1899 came the news that the doctor was dangerously ill with spinal fever. On May 31, Dr. Drake died after an illness of three weeks. He was 61 years old.

As with most newspapers of the day, the report of his last days was written in painstaking detail. "Soon after he was taken sick, Dr. Ladd of Great Falls was sent for and after his arrival Dr. Cooper of this place was called in consultation of the case at once and neither believed that the sick man had more than a fighting chance for his life from the first.

"In spite of all that medical skill, kind nursing and loving care could do, he grew worse until the fatal hour of dissolution arrived. As might be supposed from the nature of the disease, his sufferings were indescribable, though it is believed that he was unconscious during the last week of his sickness."

His obituary covered his schooling, his military service on the Union side during the Civil War, the war being the place he first contracted the cerebro-spinal fever that would kill him; his family, his career and his civic involvement after moving to Choteau in October 1893.

Having been the giver of medical services, Drake became the recipient in his last illness, and was provided with the same nurse services that he had supervised earlier. Court records show C.E. Moore was paid $40.25 to care for him. He was buried in the Choteau Cemetery.

William McBratney supplied a solid red cedar-draped, black cloth casket and outside case for $150, and flowers for $12. The probate records indicate that Drake had enough life insurance to support his wife, Celia, for many years. She died in Choteau in 1920 at age 80. Drake's colleague in

Dupuyer, Dr. Henry Gillette, sold his ranch in June 1906 and died six months later in Florida.

By 1901, the county appears to have opened a facility that was called a hospital in the newspapers, but it was basically a place to quarantine people during smallpox outbreaks. In December 1902, the county approved a year's lease at $10 per month with Mary M. Sulgrove to use the buildings on her ranch near Choteau, for use as a hospital for contagious diseases.

A year later, in September 1903, the county bought C.N. Farley's 80-acre ranch 1.5 miles north of Choteau and all the buildings for use as a poor farm and hospital. The county commissioners engaged John G. Jackson as farm steward at a salary of $35 per month, and subsistence.

It was not until May 1909 that the movement for a community hospital was in the news again when Drs. F.A. Long and H.W. Bateman announced their work to "ascertain the sentiment of the people of Choteau and vicinity with regard to a hospital to be erected in the town for the service of all the tributary territory."

8

The Legislature Creates Teton County

February 21, 28, March 7, 2018

Teton County marked its 125th anniversary on March 1, 2018, albeit without the boosterism and celebration affected by the folks in Choteau when the Legislature finally approved its creation on the fourth try in February 1893.

Those unsuccessful efforts extended back to February 1887 when "Uncle" Jesse Taylor, a co-founder of the Sands and Taylor (ST) Ranch and a representative in the Montana Territorial House, introduced the first bill to create the county of Teton out of Chouteau County, one of the nine original counties established in 1865.

Readers should note that this tale will use the spelling "Chouteau" for the county and "Choteau" for the town, although the county did not officially change its spelling, to add the inside "u," until March 5, 1903.

While the name "Teton County" starts with Taylor's bill, it was House member and Fort Shaw trader Joseph H. McKnight in early 1876, who first introduced a bill to split off the western part of Chouteau County to create a new county — "Dearborn County," with Sun River as the county seat.

The proposed new county took in all of "Lewis and Clarke" County north of Rock Creek, a slice each from Meagher and Missoula counties, and all that part of Chouteau County north and west from the mouth of Sun River, the

Helena Weekly Herald explained.

Introduced on the 23rd day of the legislative session on Jan. 25, 1876, House Bill 53 was kept alive until the 37th day when procedural motions in committee and then on the House floor, killed it.

The Hon. George Steell of Sun River in January 1877 introduced a bill to create Dearborn County from the mouth of Sun River north to the Canada line, then west to the Continental Divide, then south to the north fork of the Dearborn River, then down the Missouri River to the mouth of Sun River. The Towns and Counties Committee rejected the bill on the 40th day, the last day of the session of the Ninth Legislative Assembly.

A Benton Record reader wrote, "The Dearborn County bill had such an early and severe attack of sickness, that it is now believed to have come to an untimely end, caused by a caucus meeting of Chouteau County voters in a potato cellar. The said voters circulated a petition, the effect of which proved that they were no small potatoes."

Choteau's residents contemplated a new county in November 1884 when Sun River Sun correspondent H. Donahue wrote, "Choteau, Dearborn County's future seat, will celebrate Thanksgiving Day with horse racing, turkey shooting and a grand ball in the evening. The Sun River String Band will furnish the music. Everybody and their girls are invited and a general good time is expected."

Taylor introduced the Dearborn County bill in January 1885, with similar boundaries, but with Choteau as the proposed county seat.

This time the River Press in Fort Benton, Chouteau County's county seat, went ballistic in an all-out journalistic war on the prospect, saying in part, "To organize Dearborn County now would be to paralyze Chouteau and pauperize the residents of the proposed new county.

"Chouteau is about the only county in the territory that has no railroad within its borders, from which so much revenue in the way of taxation is derived. Why not postpone this county division business, so far as this county is concerned, until such time as the development of our resources will warrant it? Is it the part of wisdom or justice to bankrupt an existing county by taking half its meager wealth to form a new one?

"The proposed county of Dearborn is one of the schemes that not only has no merit, but contemplates an outrage of the grossest kind. Our people must be up and doing to prevent it."

The Sun countered with, "A Good Citizen of the village of Choteau says: 'We don't want a new county; our people are not in favor of it.' — River Press.

"In view of the fact that a petition, which was circulated asking for the new county, was signed by near 200 of the citizens of the valley, the aforesaid, 'Good Citizen' must be almost alone in his opinion."

On Feb. 10, the River Press noted, "The scheme is not moving smoothly and Choteau and Sun River are watching each other with a jealous eye," and the following week, it triumphantly reported, "Dearborn County is dead."

"The defeat of the Dearborn County scheme in the House was somewhat unexpected, as Mr. Jesse Taylor, the father and champion of the bill, is a member of that body. But this settles the question effectively and for two years more, at least, the matter of county division will be lost sight of," the newspaper opined.

In March 1887, Taylor was at it again, but this time, it was to create "Teton" County out of Chouteau County, with Choteau as the county seat instead of Sun River.

By that time, the village of Choteau had a newspaper, the Choteau Calumet, to counter the negative publicity in the River Press, but its work was to no avail.

"The Teton County bill was defeated in the House by a vote of 16 to six. Rep. J.F. Taylor worked tooth and nail for the bill, but was almost alone in the contest for its passage. Alderson and Kanouse, representatives of distant counties in no way affected by the bill, were among its bitterest opponents.

"Mr. Taylor deserves sincere thanks, as his action has undoubtedly the unanimous approval of this community. With such backing as the Cascade scheme possessed, any fool might have secured its success with hardly an effort, but it took brains, courage and conscientious devotion to duty to contend, almost single-handed, against an army of unscrupulous opponents for the passage of the Teton County bill," the Calumet wrote.

The citizens of Choteau tried again in February 1889, but nothing came of it. Then in January 1891, after Montana's statehood, a county division bill again was introduced. The River Press noted, however, that the bill would be opposed in the Senate on the grounds that its eastern boundary line was 12 miles east of the principal meridian, too close to Fort Benton, among other things.

More wrangling ensued, with accusations that some legislators said one thing to get elected, then voted the opposite when it came time to decide the question. In the end, the Senate killed the Teton County bill in March 1891.

The community lost Taylor as its county division advocate in May 1892, when he died in Great Falls after an illness of several months.

The Calumet had folded in 1889, but in 1890 the Montanian was born with Shuler M. Corson at the helm. The creation of Teton County was now just a matter of time, everyone, both Republicans and Democrats, believed.

Montanian readers were apprised of a new complication

in July 1892, when they learned that a townsite was to be "laid out at Dupuyer shortly, with a view, it is said, of getting the county seat of Teton County located there next winter."

In August, the paper republished a snippet from the Rising Sun newspaper in Augusta. "And such an awakening. Choteau, which in the event of the formation of the new county of Teton never dreamt of being other than the county seat, is rudely awakened from her dream of security by the presence of a formidable rival in the growing and enterprising town of Dupuyer. A mass meeting to determine the question has already been called."

Two weeks later Choteau learned, "Surveyor J.H. Day arrived from the north on Wednesday where he has been doing considerable work of late. The result of one of his trips north is the laying out of the townsite of Dupuyer for J.W. McKnight who lately moved over from Sun River. The new town occupies 40 acres, lies square with the world and on each side of the creek. The plat will be placed before the Chouteau County Commissioners at their next meeting."

The last edition of 1892 reported, "The Legislative Assembly will meet next Monday and already there is a large contingent packing their grips preparatory to storming that body in the interests of Teton County.

"Julian Burd will probably attend this session of the Legislature in the interests of Teton County, also J.W. McKnight, W.R. Ralston, Z.T. Burton, Julius Hirshberg, et al. In fact nearly all the boys will be there either in their own or somebody else's interest."

The residents of western Chouteau County said they would not take "no" for an answer this time.

"A meeting was held in Masonic Hall on last Saturday afternoon for the purpose of considering the necessary steps for looking after the passage of the Teton County bill, and looking after the interests of the town of Choteau during the approaching term of the state Legislature," the Dec. 30, 1892, Montanian reported.

The interest was statewide, for it would be the first division of Chouteau County, the "big boss county of America," (meaning the largest).

The Anaconda Standard wrote, "The people of the Teton country are anxious for a county of their own. ... They assert that politics does not figure in the movement and that they do not care whether the new county officers are 'republicans, or democrats, or Irish or Dutch or Missourians or Methodists or heathens,' but that home rule is what they want."

On Jan. 6, 1893, the Montanian reported, "Sol Cohen, J.F. Burd, Julius Hirshberg and Chas. Blackman left for Helena by private conveyance to the Falls at 12 o'clock midnight, Wednesday. They go as a committee from Teton County to lay before the Legislature a petition for county division. May their prayer be granted."

W.H. Webb and engineer J.H. Day completed a map of the proposed new county to show the assembly, "the most complete map of western Chouteau County ever gotten up."

Montanian publisher Corson mentioned one concern. "J.W. McKnight came in from Dupuyer last Friday evening on his way to Helena where he will make a strong effort to have Dupuyer named by the Legislature as the county seat of Teton County, failing in which he will oppose the formation of the new county to the best of his ability.

"This is but natural on his part, as he owns the townsite there, having purchased it for speculation, but it is terribly rough on his neighbors. Mack's interests in the proposed new county do not extend outside of the sacred precincts of his townsite; anything which would jeopardize his chances of booming Dupuyer does not meet with his approval."

People at an earlier mass meeting in Dupuyer had supported the county division, but Corson alleged that on Dec. 28, "another meeting was held, but it was not a mass meeting. A few select men assembled and disregarding the resolutions adopted in the mass meeting, they declared that they would defeat county division in case the county seat went to Choteau.

"Happily the population of the town of Dupuyer cuts but a small figure in the proposed county. There is a population of but 10 or 12 persons in the town and but nine buildings, principally owned by McKnight. Choteau, on the other hand, has an actual population of 275 and 115 buildings, principally business houses and residences."

On this, the fourth try, Fort Benton residents supported county division. Their Jan. 11 resolution said in part, "Whereas it is apparent that the residents of the western part of Chouteau County are desirous of being separated from us for the reason that their present great distance from the county seat is a matter of great personal inconvenience to the people of that section. .... Resolved, that we ... pledge ourselves not to antagonize the scheme for the formation of Teton County."

This time Sen. John W. Power from Fort Benton introduced the bill in the Senate. The boundaries were drawn nearly identical to those of the present day, except the eastern line was the principal meridian of Montana and the county extended all the way to the Canadian border, then along the border to the Continental Divide, taking in the Blackfeet Reservation.

Choteau was fixed as the county seat until a permanent place was designated by ballot at the 1894 election. The bill, set to go into effect on March 1, named the first county officers, although some were changed during the amendment process. Lastly, the residents would not be allowed to build a courthouse until the assessed valuation reached $3 million.

The news came in Sam Mitchell's telegram, "Teton County bill has passed the House and Senate." Gov. Rickards had no issue with signing it.

Finally, it was done. An elated, but over-hasty Corson offered the first notable evidence when he printed for the first time "Choteau, Teton County, Montana," below The Montanian's masthead in its Feb. 3, 1893, edition. ▰

9

Teton County Celebrates

March 14, 2018

The hard work of organizing Teton County's new government offices would take place in March 1893, but first it was time to party.

The weather was about as bad then as it has been recently, and the first date for the grand banquet was postponed until Feb. 13. The men in Choteau — no women were mentioned as being invited — celebrated the creation of Teton County at the Teton Exchange building where they also honored the Teton County Committee, "whose labors in securing the creation of the new county were so signally crowned with success at this session of the Legislature," the Montanian reported on Feb. 17.

"The seating capacity of the hall was taxed to the utmost which had but for the inclemency of the weather, been altogether too small for the accommodation of the guests. The tables were well supplied with the choicest of all the markets afford and with wines of the best vintage."

Dr. S.H. Drake opened the exercise by a request that all rise and join in singing "My Country." The Rev. R.H. Reed said grace, "after which all fell to and did ample justice to the good things which had been so excellently prepared for them by mine host of the 'Valley,' A.B. Fowler."

The menu: raw oysters, celery, olives; chicken salad, lobster salad, Sauterne wine; cold turkey with cranberry sauce, Roman punch, cold chicken with jelly, claret; cold roast pork, apple sauce, sherry wine; vanilla ice cream with assorted cakes, assorted nuts, fruits, candies, champagne, coffee and cigars.

After the disposal of the edibles, the toasts commenced, and there followed in the news a list of toasts and a name, presumably the leadership of Choteau at that time. Montana was lauded by Judge Dunlap "who in a few well chosen words made us love our state more for what he said."

The toasts: Song "My Country," company; Grace by the Rev. R.H. Reed; Our Guests, J.G. Bair; Columbia, Johan F. Burd; Montana, J.H. Dunlap; Teton County, W.R. Ralston; Our Town, T.P. Aspling; Song, George Richards; Our industries, Jesse Taylor; Harrison & Cleveland, Sol Cohen; Our governor, J.B. Mitchell; The Legislature, George Richards; Song, Reed; The ladies, A.C. Warner; Our bachelors, Clinton Fawcett; Medical profession, Dr. Wamsley; The legal profession, James Sulgrove; Our country press, S.M. Corson; Our state press, T.W. Lett; Our schools, John A. Kennedy; Irrigation, W.R. Ralston; Teton valley, James Gibson; Our newcomers, David Dowty; and Old timers, Jacob Schmidt.

When he made his toast, Wamsley recalled that Dr. Herbert Smith, a physician, had lost his life "in the cause of Teton County" in 1885 and that "his remains now lay in an unmarked grave in our cemetery. Immediately a subscription was proposed to raise a fund for the erection of a monument to his memory and a considerable sum was deposited with Warner for that purpose." That pedestal monument can be seen in the Choteau Cemetery.

Reed sang, "Don't Count Your Chickens Before They are Hatched." A committee then drew up a resolution to "express our sincere appreciation of the laudable effort of those of our citizens who devoted their time and energies to securing the passage of the Teton County bill through the Legislature."

"Taken all in all, the first banquet held at Choteau will

long be remembered by all who were so fortunate as to participate," the Montanian stated.

Not to exclude the younger generation, the Montanian on Feb 24 advertised a Teton County Ball in the Truchot & Crawford building, set for Feb. 28, the day before the county government took effect.

"Don't forget the grand ball next Tuesday evening. The young folks will go dancing out of old Chouteau into the new county of Teton. A grand inaugural! Tickets: Ball and Supper, $3."

On March 3, the news reported, "The Teton County ball last Tuesday evening when the young folks danced out of Chouteau County to Teton County was a most enjoyable affair and well attended. Supper was served by Mine Host Fowler, at the Valley restaurant, and was one of those feasts for which he is becoming famous."

Editor Corson noted on March 3, "March came in like a sullen old lion, and from the commonly accepted theory it will go out like a lamb, not, however, like a strong, healthy, frisky lamb, but like a lamb, nevertheless."

Appointed County Commissioners C. Wallace Taylor and Chas. W. Gray and Clerk and Recorder Wamsley held the first commissioners' meeting on March 8.

10

Teton County Officials Start Work

March 21, 2018

The appointed officials of Teton County began their work on March 8, 1893, and the Montanian newspaper in that month published an assorted number of "firsts" for its readers to note.

The new officers, who would serve until the November 1894 general election, were: Commissioners W.S. Clark, Chas. W. Gray and C. Wallace Taylor; Treasurer Cicero L. Bristol; Clerk and Recorder J.E. Wamsley; Sheriff Alfred Hamilton; Assessor S.F. Ralston Jr.; Clerk District Court S. McDonald; Superintendent of Schools J.G. Bair; Attorney James Sulgrove; Public Administrator Byron Corson; Surveyor J.H. Day; and Coroner S.H. Drake.

The new county was placed in the 10th Judicial District.

The Teton County Committee that promoted the county creation had one more person to thank, Judge Dudley DuBose, who drew up the bill to create the county. The gentlemen presented him with "a handsome gold-headed cane on which are engraved the words: 'Compliments of Teton County,'" the Helena newspaper reported.

Clark was not at the first commissioners' meeting when oaths and bonds were dealt with. They created two townships and two school districts (#1 and #2) within those boundaries, Choteau and Dupuyer, and four road districts. They agreed to advertise for bids for transcribing Chouteau

County records and for the maintenance and care of the poor, medicines and medical treatment. They appointed road supervisors, including Dudley Doolittle, road supervisor district 1. They fixed the sheriff's salary at $1,000 per year and appointed George Magee justice of the peace for Dupuyer Township.

Professor Bair had been the principal and teacher in the Choteau School. Once he began his duties as superintendent of schools, Mrs. Geo. Barron succeeded him for the remainder of the term. He had served for four years.

Bristol set up shop to receive applications for licenses from merchants, doctors, lawyers, saloonkeepers and others desiring to do business within Teton County.

On March 31 Ronald McDonald was the first person sent to the poor farm, and Sheriff Hamilton left that day for the asylum at Warm Springs with Mrs. Charles Lepage (nee Annie Samples) who was adjudged insane a few days earlier.

The first marriage was at the residence of R.M. Steele, on Sunday evening, March 12: Ewing Steele and Miss Emma Buss, both of Choteau, Justice Dunlap officiating. "The groom is well and favorably known in this and other parts of the state as is also his estimable bride," the paper noted.

The first child born in Teton County was on March 2, 1893, a son to Mr. and Mrs. Frank Robinson. "Mrs. Robinson has been sick for some six or eight weeks, coming here from Blackfoot for medical treatment and the fact that she has given birth to a child and that both are doing well is a pleasing announcement," the Montanian reported.

The second child, a son, was born on March 10 to the wife of Geo. Adlam.

And then, page 6 of the March 17 Montanian had this mention:

"Born on the prairie. For some weeks Mrs. Geo. Quail [nee Maggie Manix] of Sun River had been visiting her parents near Dupuyer. On Monday she and her sister came in on the northern coach and on Tuesday morning they boarded the coach for Sun River. There were six passengers on the coach, four women and two men, besides the driver. The day was raw with a northeast wind and occasionally spitting snow.

"Mrs. Quail was in a delicate condition and was on her way home, having an idea but that she had sufficient time to reach that haven of rest without difficulty. The sequel proved, however, that she had overestimated her strength and powers of endurance to stand a 60-mile stage ride over hard frozen roads and in such weather.

"When within five miles of Sun River, on the open prairie before reaching the head of Mill Coulee, it became necessary to stop the coach and a bed was made on the ground from all the wraps in the coach. One of the lady passengers remained with Mrs. Quail and her sister, the remainder of the party hastening to town where they informed Mr. Quail of the event, who at once started out with bed and bedding. Arriving on the scene, he found himself a father and everything progressing finely.

"Later reports are to the effect that the child died before reaching Sun River but that the mother was doing well." A year, almost to the day, Mrs. Quail gave birth to a healthy baby boy.

11

The County Poor

September 25, 2013

Caring for the county's poor is as old or older than the creation of Teton County, as were the taxes to support that safety net.

From the first, all able-bodied men paid a $2 annual poll tax, but a half mill was soon charged on property to support the "Poor Fund."

At the first commissioners' meeting in March 1893, they agreed to call for bids "for the maintenance and care of the poor, medicines and medical treatment for the sick, poor and infirm of this county and to the inmates of the county jail who may require medicines and medical treatment as well as for burial of paupers."

Thereafter, bids were advertised each year that developed into an annual competition sometimes within pennies of each other for the lowest-bid government contracts.

Sherman Calvin Chezum garnered the first contract for the maintenance of the county poor at the rate of $10 per week per head. A man named Ronald McDonald was the first person "sent to the poor farm," the location of which was "near Choteau" but which could not be deduced from those earliest newspaper accounts.

A New York native, Richard A. Baker, 41, was the first person to die while a county charge. He succumbed to consumption (tuberculosis) at the poor farm on Aug. 13, 1893.

Joe Arnold charged $10 to make a coffin, while it cost more to buy the first poor house entry book ($18.50).

In 1894 the commissioners purchased from the trustees of the Choteau cemetery "space for 10 graves for county paupers, to include space already occupied with graves of paupers since the creation of Teton County, the price agreed upon between trustees of Choteau cemetery and county commissioners, being $5 for each space for graves, being $50 in all."

Sometimes the newspapers marked the passing of an indigent with a note in the county commissioners' minutes: "burial at county expense," but other people whose lives ended down on their luck received poignant obituaries: "Michael Brennan, a native of Ireland, 54, May 14, 1894. In the death of Mike Brennan, "Kelly," for as such he was generally known, quite a character has been removed from among us.

"Coming to America when quite small, he joined the army and served throughout the war, and then when the great conflict was over, he continued to serve his adopted country until some 10 or 15 years ago, when he became a resident of Montana.

"Mike was as tough, physically, as a hickory whip, and had passed safely through many hardships and hairsbreadth 'scapes. The last of these was when a couple of years ago he was blown up by giant powder and slightly disfigured.

"Mike was his only and worst enemy. His only vice was whiskey. In all else he was a good man and a patriot, but, like many who served their country, he went unrewarded and finally died at the poor farm, but not until death had marked him for his own did he allow himself to become a county charge. Rest easy, Mike."

12

The Winter of 1893

March 28, 2018

The spate of crazy winter weather in early 2018 was a lot like the winter of early 1893 when the first Teton County officials were busy setting up their government offices, having the Legislature's authority to form a new county from the western part of Chouteau County.

The weather in the first week of January 1893 experienced a regular chinook that melted the ice and snow on the ranges. The Montanian newspaper noted only one accident, when one of W.S. Barrett's herders was seriously injured by being blown from a steep embankment while carrying a weakling in his arms.

"The man undertook to descend from a high rocky ridge when the strong wind caught him and hurled him down the declivity, dislocating his shoulder and bruising him severely about the body and head and leaving him lying unconscious at the foot of the hill.

"As the accident occurred at the home ranch no time was lost in caring for the injured man, but his recovery seemed slow and uncertain, and on Monday Mr. Barrett came to town for Dr. Drake, and now the shattered sheepherder is rapidly recovering from the injuries," the news reported.

The weather had its weird moments when during the second week, "Just before noon today a terrific blizzard began and lasted for less than half an hour. Had there been any snow on the ground utter darkness would have reigned. As it was, one could scarcely see across the street for a few minutes."

During the third week, the news reported that Choteau physician Jacob Wamsley, M.D., and his wife got lost all night in a snowstorm on their way from the Marias River country, but made it eventually to Choteau.

A second report noted that about six weeks earlier, Dave Able, Ed. Ranger, Charles Goodspeed and Jimmie Stone were on their way to prospect in the Sweet Grass Hills, when they "came near perishing in the storm before they got there, being compelled to burn everything they had with them which was composed of wood except their wagon, to keep from freezing."

News editor S.M. Corson reported a change in the weather. "Grass had begun to start and some few ranchers had commenced to plow for the spring seeding and the stockmen were in great glee over the prospects." On Jan. 24 the north wind suddenly sprang up lowering the temperature to eight below zero, the first time during the month. "Since then the temperature has not been above zero, except on the 27th, when it reached .5 above."

Snow began falling and continued almost uninterruptedly until Jan. 31, then it let up for one day, but the next day it started in again "and has kept it up pretty regularly ever since, so that there is now about 12 or 14 inches of snow on the ground. In some places the north wind, which has prevailed for the past 10 days, has partially blown it away, but it lies too deep on all the face of the land to allow stock feeding on the ranges.

"The weather has been so severe that no stockmen have been in town, and it is impossible at this writing to tell of any actual losses, though the mail carrier from Belleview reports that several calves and young critters were frozen to death there last Tuesday and Wednesday nights, when the temperature fell to -41 and -42, the coldest for several years past," Corson reported.

Folks were saying it was really the worst spell of weather known in this section for many years. "Stock must be suffering terrible though as stated above, no stockmen have been heard from since the storm began and no estimate can be made at this time."

Sleighing was reported good with six to eight inches of snow on the beaten track but coal and wood were very scarce in town all through February.

"It is currently reported that it was so cold at Dupuyer this week that whiskey was frozen solid and that the dealers are dispensing it by the lump," Corson quipped.

A chinook arrived for 48 hours, then the thermometer took a tumble, and the region got another two inches of snow. The pattern repeated during April as the county officials waited for contractor W. Burgy to finish the stone building they planned to rent for use as the first courthouse.

The First Courthouse

April 3, 2018

By all the news accounts, W.F. Burgy was an enterprising businessman from Great Falls when he secured the contract to build the first courtroom and county office building for Teton County officials in March 1893.

Burgy had been in Montana since at least 1889 making his money from Army contracts to supply commodities like corn, bran and wood to Fort Shaw on the Sun River.

In 1891 he operated a general book and stationary store in Great Falls that stocked schoolbooks and "monster fire crackers over a foot in length," among other things.

In 1892 he submitted bids to supply field seeds to the Blackfeet Agency on the reservation and later that year he supplied flour to the Piegan (Blackfeet) and Belknap agencies.

His first appearance in Choteau was in December 1892 when the Montanian newspaper reported that he had accepted a lumber delivery to build a new hotel at the corner of Main and Hamilton (now First Street Northwest) streets opposite the old Valley Hotel.

The Teton County Commissioners met during the first week of March to organize the new county, and then held a special meeting on March 16 to receive bids on renting office rooms. They could spend money on building a jail, but were prohibited from building a courthouse until the county's valuation reached $3 million. In the meantime, they could spend money for office rent, including their first temporary digs that the newspaper never identified.

The commissioners received four bids and Burgy won the contract by offering to furnish a courtroom and offices with a janitor and steam heat for an annual rent of $2,400 for 18 months from June 1 with the privilege of extending the contract for five years.

The building's location was between Jacob Smith's (Schmidt) residence and the new hotel on Hamilton Street with occupancy ready by June 1.

The first rock for the courthouse was delivered on April 6, and while his workers tackled the construction, Burgy ran unsuccessfully for the mayoral office in Great Falls. The commissioners granted him a 15-day extension at the same meeting they asked for bids to construct the jail.

By April 1893 Choteau had 255 buildings, one bank, several stores, two livery stables, two hotels, the courthouse block under construction, also a brick hotel; a "good graded school," and wagon, butcher, blacksmith, carpenter, harness, shoemaker and paint shops; two physicians, two lawyers and two newspapers.

McKenzie and Hunter had the subcontract for the rockwork on the courthouse building, and the newspaper noted their progress.

"The men on the courthouse building purchased a stove the other day and put it up in their sleeping quarters. In building a fire, the fuel was put into the oven instead of the fireplace. As a result the 'blasted thing had no draft' and soon filled the room with smoke. Hunter wanted to pitch it out doors, but Sandy saw the mistake and soon had the thing in running order."

By May 5, the courthouse foundation was completed and the walls were being put up as fast as rock could be delivered. The rock came from Priest's Butte, as this article shows. "The blowing up of Priest's Butte which was to have come off last week, did not occur until Wednesday of this week, owing to the failure of the powder to arrive until that date. Hundreds of perch of rock were blown down the side of the hill but the hole made is not noticeable at all. It is estimated that there is enough rock in this butte to build all the buildings at present in Montana."

On June 16, the news was, "Today the masons are laying the last rock on the courthouse building. A flagstaff now surmounts the apex of an ornamental cornice, and from which 'Old Glory' will be flung to the breeze on the Fourth of July."

Rather than explain that Burgy missed the June 16 deadline for occupancy, the Montanian offered the news that the nation's birthday, July 4th, was celebrated in Choteau with orations and foot races and, "The day was ushered in with the burning of much powder and explosions of numerous sticks of giant. Flags were unfurled from every flagstaff in town, and from the housetops. From the flagstaff on the new courthouse building proudly floated the first flag ever raised in Teton County."

Four years later, the rented courthouse burned down, but that's another story.

14

Community Band

June 25, 2014

Acantha editor and Choteau Community Band organizer Melody Martinsen penned the band's motto, "A Tradition Worth Preserving," decades ago, she said recently, but readers might be surprised how far back that tradition extends.

"At last Choteau is the proud possessor of a brass band, and one that will be able to make music too, in a very short time," the Montanian newspaper reported on Feb. 16, 1894. The 14-piece Choteau Brass Band, also called the Choteau Cornet Band, had organized in January with Wolf Burton as music director and experienced Dupuyer musician A.J. Vance as the instructor. They secured subscriptions to pay for the instruments and had collected $132 in a month.

The band's debut occurred at the Literary Society's Feb. 16 meeting, where the members "elicited the warmest applause" and were "looked upon with pride by all our people."

"To the sweet strains of music which this band will dispense upon the ambient air, Choteau will march on to her great destiny and greatness," the Montanian wrote.

Its music graced events for a time, then it faded away as organizations tend to do over time, but the idea was born that Choteau should have a community band. The Acantha boasted at each reorganization of a new band and praised each new set of volunteers as the years went by.

The first mention of the Choteau band playing on July 4 occurred in 1904.

Dubbed "one of the best bands in northern Montana," the band was on hand for the opening of the Weaver saloon in December 1913. It opened the rally of the Republican campaign for Teton County in October 1914, and rendered lively music at the newly formed local militia's meetings of the National Guard that year.

With the intention of giving concerts on Sunday mornings on the streets of Choteau, weather permitting, the band reached a new height. Music Director John Holland sought to increase the 20-piece band by creating a beginner's band.

They proudly entertained the crowd at the commemoration of the first community Christmas tree held in town in December 1915 and gave dances all around the county, some for free, others to raise operating funds.

At yet another band reincarnation when America declared war on Germany in 1917, 500 people gathered in the high school auditorium to hear patriotic addresses and several selections by the band and the high school girls' Glee Club.

When each newly conscripted contingent of Teton County's soldier boys assembled at the train station in Choteau, the Choteau band was there to entertain them and the townsfolk who saw them off.

A quarter-page ad in the June 20, 1918, Acantha announced the largest July 4th celebration ever attempted in Teton County, with proceeds to benefit the Red Cross and music by the Choteau Band. Besides races, minstrel shows, a dance, a parade and the smallest stallion in the world on display, Madame Burnett, fortuneteller, was on hand with "advice that will help you all your life."

The Acantha deemed the celebration a success "in every way" with $1,800 added to the Red Cross's treasury and no complaints regarding the entertainment.

15

The Acantha Marks 100-plus Years in the Publishing Business

September 7, 14, 21 and 28, 2005, Jan. 1, 2014

September 2005 marked the 111th anniversary of the Acantha, whose name is a botanical word that refers to a spine, thorn or prickle, and its 101st year of continuous operation in Choteau.

The Acantha was first published in Dupuyer on Sept. 15, 1894. The publishers said they established the paper in Dupuyer because the community was the near-geographic center of newly-formed Teton County. They advocated Dupuyer for the permanent county seat over Choteau, the temporary one, and Helena over Anaconda for the permanent capital of Montana.

The competing newspaper in Choteau, the Montanian, nicknamed the Acantha: the Dupuyer Prickly Pear. Various accounts over the years say that the Acantha was a thorn in the side of the politicians, but the first publishers never stated why they chose the unique name.

Certainly, the newspaper was a prickle to the Montanian, competing in every way even as it lost the election to have Dupuyer named the county seat.

The Acantha changed hands five times during its 10-year sojourn in Dupuyer. It was a time when stagecoaches advertised and the news included the building of the First Methodist Church in Choteau. For $1.5 million the Piegan Indians ceded the land that would become Glacier

National Park. The Burton Creamery opened, then closed with $3,000 in debt, but Fryers Lumber was offering lumber outside the mouth of the North Fork of the Teton Canyon to meet the housing needs for the growing communities along the Rocky Mountain Front.

The Choteau Telephone Exchange had 41 subscribers in 1897 and the users were warned to "insert the lightning plug on top of the telephone during storms. By doing this there is no danger of lightning escaping in the room."

In 1898, St. Luke (now St. Joseph) Catholic Church was dedicated and John Zimmerman advertised his expertise at drilling artesian wells. That year the Acantha and the Montanian were in a nasty fight over who said what in the last political election.

In 1899, readers learned that the City Drug Store, which housed the post office, was now "brilliantly lighted" at night by acetylene gas instead of coal oil lamps.

In 1901, the Dupuyer Acantha publisher, George Magee, complained that more Dupuyer news was published in the columns of the Montanian and Chronicle (the Choteau newspaper) than could be found in the Acantha.

Then in early 1904, the local-newspaper world was buzzing with the news. Longtime Montanian publisher Charles Trescott, who had sold the Montanian to T.J. Lowman in February with the promise that he would retire, reversed his decision. Trescott and his brother, Bert, bought the Dupuyer Acantha printing press and subscription list and moved the same to Choteau. They did not reset the volume numbers, but continued the newspaper as Vol. 10, No. 29, dated March 24, 1904.

Lowman attacked the Trescotts in his editorials, but the latter responded that the "vulgar and obscene insinuations only serve to show the mental deficiency of the writer." Eventually the Montanian stopped publication.

Charles Trescott raised the subscription price to $2 per year, up one dollar under the prior management. He faithfully reported on Choteau's progress until he sold the paper in 1907 to Prof. A.B. Guthrie, who had been the principal of Teton County Free High School for six years.

The Acantha changed hands again in April 1913, when Guthrie retired. C.G. and Max B. Bishop, formerly of Elkader, Iowa, bought the Acantha plant and subscription list, stating they were "assuming control of a strong and live paper that is an important factor in the growth and development of the town and surrounding country."

They were also mindful that in Guthrie, the Acantha "has had an efficient and capable manager and only by exerting ourselves to the utmost and by the hearty cooperation of the people of this locality may that standard be maintained and brought higher."

Clinton Bishop showed a talent for understatement and satire after he and his brother bought the Choteau Acantha.

In his first month as the new owner, he wrote, "Wanted — An editor who can read, write and argue politics, and at the same time be religious, funny, scientific and historical at will, write to please everybody, know everything without asking or being told, always having something good to say about everybody else, live on wind and make more money than enemies. For such a man a good opening will be made (in the graveyard)."

The top news story in May 1913 described how the powers that be planned to build a 320-mile-long "park-to-park road" between Yellowstone and Glacier national parks, now known as U.S. Highway 89.

In June 1913, Bishop installed a new linotype machine, a major investment. The Mergenthaler Linotype Co. "Model K" was the best machine of its kind for a small office, Bishop wrote.

The Bishops garnered the lucrative county publishing contract, only to find that on July 4, and to everyone's surprise, former Acantha owner Charles Trescott and his son, Richard, came back to town and established "The Choteau Montanan."

Although the regional newspapers wished Trescott well on their editorial pages, Bishop made no mention of his new competitor.

Early in 1915, Max Bishop took over the daily running of the Acantha, about the time that the Teton County Commissioners were in a nasty court fight over the division to create Pondera County.

In January 1916, the Acantha along with several merchants sponsored a Grand Piano and Popularity Contest where one could nominate a favorite young lady from Choteau or an adjoining town.

The award committee tallied votes on the basis of the number of new Acantha subscribers and renewals. New subscribers paid $1.75 and received a coupon for 600 votes, but 10-year subscriptions at $17 received a coupon for 12,500 votes. Local merchants offered a 25-vote coupon for each $1 cash purchase.

By the time the contest ended, the Acantha had 200 new subscribers and "considerable money through the paying up of subscriptions and we feel much gratified at the result of the contest," the writer said.

The fortunate girl to win the $400 piano with 567,850 votes was the niece of the Acantha's competitor. Hazel Trescott was an accomplished musician and a Choteau schoolteacher.

On Sept. 5, 1917, the Acantha reported that the county's first contingent of 10 men to meet its quota for the army left for basic training. "The departure of the boys has brought the war home to the people in a very direct way, as the function in their honor last evening demonstrated. The boys left with absolute confidence and assurance of the loyalty and support of the folks at home where prayers and good wishes will accompany them through every circumstance of war," the writer said.

The Acantha changed owners in the midst of the Spanish-influenza epidemic and World War I. Ernest L. "Bees" Jourdonnais, who had worked on and off at the Acantha since 1906, bought the paper in November 1918.

He set about reporting on the news, and made his philosophy known through effective editorials. "The Acantha is politically independent and owes nor offers undivided allegiance to no political party or organizations. The Acantha believes that a newspaper owes to the community it serves a conscientious effort to act at all times for the best interest of that community."

He assured readers that "when mistakes are made, as they inevitably will be, they will at least be made in good faith."

The Acantha's rival had been a keen competitor during this time, but the Choteau Montanan suffered a mortal blow in August 1921, when the elder Trescott died after a long illness. His wife and son continued to run the newspaper until Jan. 8, 1925, when they announced, "With this week the plant, business and subscription list of the Choteau Montanan pass to the ownership of The Choteau Acantha and we write '30' to our newspaper endeavor in Teton County."

Jourdonnais announced that the Acantha was now the oldest established newspaper in Teton County and that the Acantha publisher would henceforth "devote the paper less to politics and more to the upbuilding and development of this community."

Alas, a political faction rose up in opposition to the

Acantha in 1925, and Trescott's brother, Bert, established the Teton Independent, which ran for five years, before it folded.

In keeping with Jourdonnais's stated mission, the Acantha sponsored a contest in which Alva Larson, the beautiful 20-year-old daughter of Norwegian-born state Sen. Thomas Larson (R-Teton County), won the title of Teton County "Princess." She competed for the "Queen of Petrolia" crown in Helena in a contest conducted by the International Petroleum Exposition.

On Sept. 24, 1925, the top story detailed how the first snowfall of the season had left a trail of destruction. It "attacked this territory in all its fury, ripping great branches off the city's shade trees, leveling street-light poles and wreaking such havoc with the Montana Power Co.'s line southwest of Fairfield that Choteau was without power or light juice from midnight Friday until noon Wednesday." The storm also decimated the rest of the state.

In contrast to the severe weather four years earlier, Jourdonnais wrote about the "Fire Menace" in August 1929. A weed fire had occurred northwest of the high school building the week before. It "forcefully brings to mind the danger from fire that exists at this time of drought. The presence of all these dead weeds in and around Choteau is a constant menace and they should be destroyed," he wrote.

The 1920s were a time of peace, prosperity and prohibition, but Jourdonnais found fault in at least one aspect of the "Noble Experiment." He noted in an editorial that it took the federal government 10 years to issue an order that federal agents "must equip their machines with identifying insignia in order that the public and especially those driving motor cars may distinguish a federal officer from a highway robber."

On Oct. 24, 1929, the stock market crashed, launching

the Great Depression. The Acantha weathered the storm due in large part to its reliance on a largely agricultural economy. It dedicated its Sept. 19, 1935, issue to the 4-H club members and to their teachers, the council and sponsors.

In September 1936, the Acantha reported that about 1,400 students in Teton County were back to school, up from 1,358 in 1935. Notably, nearly the same —1,311 — number of students attended school in September 2005.

On Jan. 1, 1939, Jourdonnais sold the Acantha to Iowa-native Karl Bishop, the nephew of Max Bishop. He said it was with great regret that he left the helm of the Acantha, but that he felt in need of a rest after 32 years of association with the paper. He wrote that Howard Cunningham, printer and linotype operator, would retain his present position but that Millard Bullerdick, who had been associated with the Acantha as associate editor for 11 years, would no longer be connected with the Acantha.

Jourdonnais said Bullerdick "has no immediate plans for the future," but by June 1939, Bullerdick had established a new Acantha rival, "The Teton Citizen" with his wife, Geneva.

Karl Bishop's first order of business was to explain that his desire to live in the West was kindled during a visit to Montana in 1933.

He added, "All I am going to say is that I like it here and am sure that as time goes on I'll like it all the better. There's an indescribable freer feeling in the West, a noticeable lack of pessimism and abject poverty, which coupled with the scenery and outdoor activities make it a very pleasant place to live."

Bishop's first editorial was about editorials. He called them "throwbacks to pioneer days when editors of the few newspapers in the country were regarded as wells of wisdom, sages whose knowledge and understanding of contemporary affairs gave them license to direct the thoughts and action of the masses into proper channels."

He lamented that in recent years much of the editors' creative writing, though sincere, had become extremely questionable and not always right. He said that there are two sides to every question, and that citizens in modern times, with a fund of information of their own at their disposal, are in most cases able to decide for themselves what should be done or enacted to raise the human standard of living.

He concluded, "After a year or two we may offer our humble opinion on civic affairs and in the meantime will hold our line of thought to general subjects and let the bricks fall where they may."

Then life and the Japanese changed his plans. In the Dec. 11, 1941, Acantha edition, he devoted five paragraphs to his thoughts, saying that editorial comment was just and due.

He began, "Life takes strange quirks. A week ago, we were enjoying a semi-blissful state of existence. Sunday noon came the electrifying news of treacherous Japanese aggression.

"It seems incongruous this Tuesday evening, Dec. 9, 1941, while this is being written, that many people would be still entertaining in their minds the homely holiday spirit as it has always been known here, while our President, Franklin D. Roosevelt, was making an unprecedented historic message on the present conflict."

Bishop added that it was regretful that Montana's own Jeannette Rankin cast the only dissenting vote on Congress's state-of-war declaration. "The general thought from this area is that it was a disgraceful expression of sentimentality, and one not in keeping with the state's history and lifelong tradition," he wrote.

Fate intervened again, when Bishop drew the No. 1 spot when the selective-service law first went into effect. He decided to enlist in the U.S. Army instead, and in September 1942, he sold the Acantha to Bullerdick, who, under the terms of the sales contract, agreed to discontinue publishing The Teton Citizen.

Bullerdick's announcement read in part, "Naturally, it is with a certain feeling of sorrow that I bring life of The Teton Citizen to an end. The Acantha having been established for so many years, my own judgment and that of my friends and counselors has been to preserve that paper. My hope is that I can, in a small way at least, have something to do toward publishing a good weekly newspaper in this locality." Bullerdick thanked his Citizen subscribers. He noted that Elmer "Eric" Erickson would continue in the Acantha's employ and that Choteau High School senior Donald Nordhagen, who had been working part-time with him on the Citizen since it started, would transfer to the Acantha.

Bullerdick bought the Choteau Acantha in the midst of a world war and at the halfway point in the newspaper's history.

Rationing, war bonds and the work of the Civilian Defense Corps were important newsmakers. So was the Choteau Lions Club that held its Days of '49 fundraiser for the swimming pool.

Bullerdick wrote about the men and women in uniform in 1944 along with a report that the Teton Memorial Hospital Association had filed its incorporation papers. The community began to raise funds to aid in the post-war construction of the hospital.

Bullerdick's reign as publisher came to an abrupt end when on Jan. 3, 1946, the Acantha announced that Bullerdick was starting a newspaper in another town. George and Marie Coffey had approached Bullerdick with a proposition that he found difficult to refuse. The Coffeys wanted to buy the Acantha for their son and journalism-school graduate, Jere, to run. If Bullerdick declined the offer, the Coffeys intended to build a new building, and start their own newspaper.

By 1946, the Acantha plant machinery was old and at some point would need a large infusion of cash to update. Having just come through the war, Bullerdick was in no position to do that, nor did he want to have a repeat of the era when two competing newspapers vied for advertising dollars in Choteau.

Bullerdick sold the Acantha to the Coffeys and 25-year-old Jere Coffey became editor. His "Coffey Hour" column was a mix of views, reviews and interviews.

In his first column, he wrote on behalf of mostly youthful endeavors. It was a poignant wish list since he had been confined to a wheelchair at birth and could participate in few of the activities.

Coffey wanted a new hospital like in Conrad, the reorganization of the Teton all-star baseball team, the organization of a city band and intramural softball leagues for all adult players who wanted to participate. He wanted to see the formation of an adult all-county theatre group, talent plays, tennis tournaments and swimming contests in the Lions Club pool.

With his companion and caregiver, Pat Campbell, who lifted him up the steps of the Acantha office, among other things, Coffey set about upgrading the Acantha's plant and writing about the news of the day. His editorial in September 1946 urged the county commissioners to pave Teton Canyon Road. He wrote other editorials about a Hutterite Colony's plans to buy land in Teton County.

In September 1950, the new hospital was finished and the problems of deer damage to cropland were front-page news.

The state game commission backed down on opening Teton County east of Range 8 to a special three-day hunting season. Two hundred ranchers and sportsmen filled the courthouse assembly room to protest the opening of a hunting area in the southwest section of the county. They said life and property would be placed in jeopardy.

The game commission apologized, stating that it made an error in not meeting with a representative group of Teton County before its action in opening the season.

In September 1954, the Acantha ran the obituary of former Acantha publisher A.B. Guthrie Sr. He had served as the first Teton County High School principal until 1907 and died on the opening day of school in 1954.

By 1953, Coffey had left Choteau to live where the Coffeys spent winters in Phoenix, Arizona. He left the running of the newspaper to Elmer Erickson and later Jerry Strauss. In May 1960, Coffey died at the age of 39. Strauss eulogized Coffey. "He was a good man to know," he said.

Jere Coffey was born in Choteau in 1920 and graduated from Teton County High School in 1938. Physical disabilities kept him in a wheelchair from birth until he died.

He majored in journalism in college and his wealthy parents (his father was a lawyer and had served as mayor of Choteau) purchased the Acantha for him in late 1945. He remained publisher, but turned the editor post over to Erickson in 1953 when he moved to Phoenix, earned a degree in psychology and took a job in public relations for Goodwill Industries. He died after a short illness.

Strauss, who took over from Erickson in July 1958, in his editorial reflected on Coffey's life.

He said, "When a person is burdened with a serious physical handicap, a handicap that will continue throughout life, there are three attitudes that may develop. The person frequently withdraws from the world almost completely and merely exists. Or, the person may lean on the handicap, capitalize on it, use it as an excuse for not attaining success. Or, the person can rise above the handicap, become an individual who willingly, accepts help from those offering it, in order to mold himself into someone who offers a definite contribution to the world in which he must live for a time."

Strauss said Coffey was the latter type — he showed by his actions that he realized his greatest potential lay in the development of his mind. Having wealthy parents helped to bring out his special abilities, and he channeled his energies into a worthwhile endeavor, Strauss said, the dissemination of news and information to the residents of this area by means of a newspaper.

It was with a confident farewell that Jere's parents, George and Marie Coffey, announced that they had sold the Acantha to Richard (Dick) Nordhagen on Dec. 29, 1960.

"His faithful and efficient service ever since the publication was taken over from Millard Bullerdick by the late Jere Coffey in 1945 has made him highly qualified to assume the role he shall now have," the Coffeys wrote.

They added, "It has been the policy of the Acantha to serve the public interest by honest and accurate coverage of the news with fairness and goodwill toward all. The success it has had has been largely due to reciprocal goodwill and cooperation of its readers without which no newspaper can render the service its readers deserve."

Nordhagen had worked at the Acantha since he was 14 years old. He hired Robert Amick as editor and would later make a practice of hiring young men and women just out of "J-school" to be editors. He introduced a young Don LaBaugh to the printing trade where he became an expert on running a commercial press.

The Acantha survived the June 1964 flood when Choteau was inundated with water and nearly all the newsprint was ruined. In the aftermath, the Acantha editorial began with "Forget Fingerpointing," and said Choteau came out of the flood in "really good shape" because "we were lucky and we had many organizations functioning well and efficiently almost from the start."

The Acantha advocated the creation of one organization trained to swing into action immediately at the threat of emergency, a central authority from which all other agencies would take orders.

By 1972, the county had published "In Time of Emergency," a citizens' handbook on nuclear attack and natural disaster that listed all the shelters in Teton County.

Nordhagen brought the newspaper up to modern times in May 1974 when he installed a new offset "cold-type" machine and retired the lead-based "hot-type" linotype machine and press.

Like 10 other area weeklies, the Acantha was no longer printed "in-house." The Shelby Promoter's new offset press did the job in an hour, although getting the newspaper "negatives" to Shelby was nearly a three-hour round trip. Nordhagen increased the subscription price to $5.20 to partially offset the added costs.

Also in 1974, the community received a grant to build a new hospital and its foundation was laid in August 1976.

With the change from the labor-intensive weekly printing of the newspaper, Nordhagen turned his energy to commercial printing, writing and to hiring other writers. In August 1978, Jeanette Rasmussen wrote a story about the baby dinosaur discovery west of Choteau.

Six years later, the "wanton killing" of a grizzly bear by an "unknown assailant" at Eureka Lake made front-page news.

Nordhagen decided to sell the Acantha after having open-heart surgery in the fall of 1989. He was 61 and reluctantly chose to retire. He sold the Acantha to Jeff and Melody Martinsen in July 1990. By that time, the Acantha sported a full-time printer and photographer, a part-time copy editor and two part-time news clerks.

The new owners, both 24, brought a new generation of journalism to the 96-year-old newspaper.

When longtime Acantha publisher Nordhagen sold the newspaper business to the Martinsens, he took a leap of faith, said Acantha co-owner Jeff Martinsen during an interview to mark the Acantha's 111th anniversary in September 2005.

"Dick called us and our lives were unalterably changed. It was a blur. We met, talked and looked at the books," Melody said.

"The staff was in place. It was a very stable business and our degrees matched the needs of the business," Jeff said.

On July 1, 1990, the Martinsens, both 24, bought the Acantha. The 1983 graduates of Choteau High School, who had married in May 1989 and settled in Great Falls, made plans to move to Choteau.

"We were given a rare opportunity at our age. We could not have gone to a bank for a loan. Dick and Joan (Nordhagen) made it happen. Dick entrusted us to pay him through a contract for deed. It was a leap of faith," Jeff said. After the sale, Nordhagen came in frequently for six months to help in the transition.

Jeff came up from Great Falls before the sale to learn the printing side of the business. Melody stayed working at the Great Falls Tribune until the last minute.

"I only had two years of working under experienced editors," Melody explained, but during that time she had chalked up several awards. In addition, she was awarded the

1987 Outstanding Graduate of the University of Montana School of Journalism.

The plan was for Melody to handle the news and editorial responsibilities. Jeff, a former smokejumper with the U.S. Forest Service, and a bookkeeper since August 1989 for Montana Ironworks and Excavating, would be responsible for the business, advertising and commercial printing aspects. He had graduated in 1987 from Western Montana College in Dillon with a bachelor's degree in business and an associate degree in personnel management.

In 1990, the Acantha was located in the small building one lot west of the present U.S. Post Office in Choteau. The building still bears the Acantha name, although it is very faint. The glass front counter held office supplies, but it was no match for the big preacher from Augusta who came in one day during Nordhagen's tenure and accidentally thumped too hard on the counter which cracked the tempered glass.

The front part of the building was filled with supplies, a few desks, the layout table and the safe. A variety of publishing, printing and folding machines consumed the rear section along with a stairway to the basement. The basement held more supplies, a darkroom, some developing equipment and a tiny bathroom.

Jeff and Melody made a temporary move to Bynum until they found a home in Choteau, but that was too far away during the first days as the new Acantha owners. "We didn't go home. We stayed in Grandpa (Earl) Thompson's camper that was parked in the Choteau City Park for the July 4th celebration," Melody recalled.

Their first edition was stressful and difficult to put together, Melody said. They immediately taught themselves how to use a computer program to set ads, but the little Macintosh computer crashed at the worst times. Melody lost at least one whole story she had written.

The July 4th newspaper sported the following message to the community, "We plan to continue the tradition of quality job printing and prompt, competent service established by Dick Nordhagen over the years. We also intend to bring readers of the Acantha expanded news coverage in a professional manner featuring fair, accurate, unbiased news accounts of the local events that affect Teton County residents."

By then, the Acantha was developing black and white photographs instead of shipping them to and from Great Falls for processing. Longtime Acantha employee Don La-Baugh did most of the printing and photography work.

The Acantha owners became active in the Montana Newspaper Association in 1991. Fellow editors were mentors to the Martinsens. In 1992, the Acantha won nine MNA awards and four first-place honors for stories written in 1991. It continues to receive awards every year.

On Jan. 12, 1994, the Acantha held an open house at its new location, 216 First Ave. N.W., Choteau. The building had been an apartment, a credit union and a daycare center before the Martinsens bought it. It had been a mortuary, originally, with easy access at ground level.

The Acantha received both praise and scorn from readers as the look of the paper evolved. The page layout changed from the horseshoe system of ads to a modified-block system. Readers who had been accustomed to the old style objected to the loss of the "banner ads" across the top of the page.

Melody instituted the "only-news-once" rule. Expanded news coverage that detailed local government activities squeezed the community-bulletin board of social events, and readers complained.

"I had a great expectation that elected officials would

behave the same ways as the ones I encountered at the state level, Melody recalled. "I discovered some officials did not understand the Open Meetings Law," she said. With a few exceptions, they were willing to learn what they needed to do to comply with the law.

The Acantha eventually converted to a digital operation.

"Don (LaBaugh) has done an awesome job," Jeff said, describing the way the veteran photographer adapted to the digital age. "Printing is done on the worst grade of paper in the world. To get a quality image, Don jumped in with both feet."

While the Acantha embraced new technology in-house, the newspaper "grids" were still hand carried to Shelby for printing. That changed in April 2001, when a snowstorm closed the road to Shelby. On a Tuesday evening, Jeff, following a back-up plan, used the Internet to send the newspaper grids electronically to the Great Falls Tribune's printing plant. "We never went back to Shelby," Jeff said. "We are now completely digital."

Commercial printing has changed with the addition of do-it-yourself technology and printers on every office desk. The Acantha does not print as many short runs as it once did, but it still prints a wide range of two- and three-part forms on pressure-sensitive paper, business cards and newsletters, to name a few.

Following in a role that Nordhagen enjoyed, Melody became a mentor to summer interns who worked at the Acantha.

Her first in-depth stories about Teton Medical Center in 1991 and 1992 are among the highlights of her list of news stories that have had an important impact on the community. The stories earned the Montana Newspaper Association's community-service award.

"The hospital was teetering on the edge of extinction. It

was so important. They had to find a way to make it work," she said. A dedicated group of community leaders worked tirelessly to keep TMC open, she said.

Other vivid stories involved trauma, death and sadness. "I covered all those things," she said, including the story of two brothers. While playing with a gun, one boy accidentally killed the other. The family came to the Acantha and told Melody to print the truth. Their wish was a gift to her and an opportunity to educate the community. It was in sharp contrast to another incident in which a family threatened her over the coverage of a fatal alcohol-related car accident.

Melody continues to grapple with news coverage seeking a balance when more goes on in the community than can ever be covered in print. She said she would continue to publish stories that inform citizens who create a dialog with local officials. "You cannot solve problems, if you don't know the issues or if the local paper is not telling you what are the alternatives," she said.

"We plan to stick around," Jeff said at the end of the interview. He said the Acantha in its 111 years of existence has shown resilience, an ability to adapt to the changing economy and new technology. "We hope we are around for another 100 years."

Valentine's Day

February 11, 2015

Valentine's Day, coming as it does in dreary February, is associated with decorated shoeboxes, heart-shaped containers of chocolate and red-tinted flowers. Around Choteau, it also was an occasion to have a good time for a good cause.

The Montanian on Jan. 4, 1895, reported, "The band boys, who by the way are always on hand at the right time, are making preparations for a 'Calico Ball,' to be given the evening of St. Valentine's Day. Already the decree has gone forth that this is to be the swell event of the season, don't cher know, and we may expect something grand."

In 1914, Choteau Drug Co. offered "red hearts in many sizes and designs, a assortment of rare beauty and value," as well as 50 designs of St. Valentine's Day postcards. Rexall Drug Store had a large advertisement for its "very attractive assortment" that was "very inexpensive."

During the war in 1918, the Belleview correspondent reported that a concert and box social with a St. Valentine party would be held at the Kalma schoolhouse (about 18 miles southwest of Choteau.) The proceeds went to the Red Cross.

By 1929, the Post Tavern was advertising heart-shaped boxes of chocolates and in 1936 the shop's ad read, "Remember your friends or relatives or sweetheart with a heart-shaped box filled with Johnson's delicious chocolates, also greeting cards."

In 1942, the emphasis was on the war, and the ads suggested, "On Valentine's Day, Remember Uncle Sam Too. Also give U.S. Defense Bond Stamps."

In keeping with the view to ration certain foods, the Household news column, listed recipes for a Valentine's Day supper party with a cake made in a heart-shaped pan with rose-tinted seven-minute frosting.

In 1950, the Choteau Parent Teacher Association used the day for a basket social and dance, the proceeds to be used for the purchase of high school band uniforms. The basket auction raised $141.85 for the band, one of the few in the state without uniforms.

Advertising for Valentine's Day increased, and by 1960 Teton Pharmacy was selling Valentine cards and heart-shaped chocolates, Choteau Drug was selling Whitman's chocolates and J.C. Penney's and Safeway were selling "Truly Fine Nylons," two pair for $1.49, for one's sweetheart.

Choteau's florists embraced the day in 1964 with a "Say It With Flowers" ad from Choteau Floral and Greenhouses. The Villager offered a complete line of Hallmark valentines and a raffle for a free sweetheart steak dinner for two to be served Valentine's Day at the Tree Top Restaurant upstairs.

Choteau Drug had a large ad for Russell Stover Candies for Valentine's Day in 1970, while the Agawam Social Club chose to make popcorn balls to be sent to the Montana Children's Home at Twin Bridges.

Also that year, several friends of some Teton County Nursing Home residents put on a Valentine's party in the gaily-decorated dining room. The Acantha reported, "As soon as the old time music started, residents who hadn't joined in for treats, came to listen." A resident expressed the sentiments of all when he said they could sit there all day and listen to the music.

Alas, St. Valentine's Day sometimes falls on Ash

Wednesday, like it did in 1923. The Rev. H.W. Bush of St. Stephen's Church, (Protestant Episcopal) reminded Acantha readers that the day introduces the season of Lent, that portion of the year, which is used to direct the attention of each believer upon the status of his own faith. The minister warned that a person who does not use the time to take stock of his character is in the same boat as the businessman who takes no annual inventory. "He has no definite knowledge of his position in the realm of the higher values," Bush said. That piece of chocolate should come second.

— 17 —
Choteau's Catholic Church

July 20, 27, August 3, 10, 17, 2016

Where people go, religious services are not far behind, and so it was that the Roman Catholic settlers along the Rocky Mountain Front hoped they could persuade Bishop John Baptist Brondel of the Diocese of Helena to send them a priest on a regular basis.

The new diocese had been formed in 1882, but priests were no strangers to the Front. Catholic missions, under the ministration of priests from the Society of Jesus, the Jesuits, were frequent missionaries to the various Indian tribes, and by 1889, they were building a school and brick church on the Blackfeet Reservation at "Piegan."

The Jesuits had tried to minister to the Blackfeet at a place near Priest Butte (from where it gets its name), but that only lasted a few months, whereupon the mission was moved to the south several times. It eventually became the St. Peter's Mission near Cascade. Couples who wanted to be married by a priest traveled to St. Peter's.

Brondel arrived in Helena in 1884, and he worked to increase the number of secular priests throughout Montana Territory. Augusta was the first community to invite the bishop to dedicate its church on June 25, 1896.

In April 1897 the Catholics in Choteau, led by Dr. Henri Beaupre, began a subscription for the purpose of building a Catholic church.

In July, the Catholics in Dupuyer did the same thing and garnered $340 almost immediately, according to an

April article in the Dupuyer Acantha. The Jesuit priest, the Rev. P. Prando, ministered in Dupuyer while he lived on the reservation. The merchant trader, J.W. McKnight, who was in charge of the subscription list, donated $100 and two lots on which to build a church.

By Aug. 12, 1897, Dupuyer Catholics had raised $585, and Prando said that $200 more would be a sufficient guarantee to commence building.

Acantha publisher C.E. Trescott in Dupuyer was confident. He wrote on Aug. 26, "Dupuyer without doubt or braggadocio is undoubtedly destined to be, not only the county seat of Teton County, but one of the largest towns in northern Montana.

"With the opening of the mineral strip of the Blackfoot reserve will come hundreds of people to this section, some of whom will settle on the government lands adjacent to this place. When the strip is thrown open it will be a part of Teton County, and Dupuyer, which is centrally located and having a better country tributary to it than Choteau, will not only be the county seat, but will be the basis of supplies for the miners operating on this end of the strip.

"The strip will probably not be opened up until next spring, although there is rumor to the contrary. However, let us not wait for that. If there was no strip, it would not alter the fact that Dupuyer is to be the largest town in Teton County, and that in the very near future. In a couple of months' time we expect to see the town hall and Catholic church completed, and the foundation laid to a 'greater Dupuyer.'"

McKnight invited bids for the Dupuyer church on Jan. 10, 1898, but was confronted in December by a lack of funds to finish it.

Choteau Catholics, meanwhile, were moving ahead with their church. On Jan. 21, 1898, the church trustees invited bids to move the old Choteau schoolhouse to lots donated by Sam Mitchell, from the opposite side of the street (now Second Avenue Northwest) to the new location (just north of First Street Northwest) to face west on lot 4, block 9.

Contractors Kelly and Boutellier moved the building by February's end. The Montanian reported, "And now the old building looms up like a veritable church on its new foundation, which is considerably higher than the old one. The building has been turned over to the committee, and just as soon as more money can be raised, it will be fitted up, seated, and put in shape for dedication as a place of worship for the Catholic members of our community and neighborhood."

In March 1898, Montanian publisher S.M. Corson credited devout Catholic Peter Joyce with guiding the project and then listed the people who contributed funds.

Corson noted $560 collected and $528 paid out: school building, $300; moving it and labor on foundation, $185; E.F. Riley, labor, $3; J.E Low, lumber, $35; and Olaf Fjeld, surveying, $5.

By June 1898, Choteau had a Catholic church very nearly completed. The altar and other trappings, including an "artificial Jesus," were in, but the pews were delayed.

Dupuyer, meanwhile, was having a difficult time finishing its Catholic edifice. Dupuyer Acantha publisher Trescott, with a hint of frustration, said, "Rev. George Logan has been returned to Choteau as pastor of the M.E. church for another year. This insures regular services at Choteau and Burton, but until the Catholic church is built at Dupuyer the ungodly in this neighborhood will stand a poor show of being led into the straight and narrow path. Bro. Logan does not seem to like Dupuyerites. You know."

Then the dedication of St. Luke's church in Choteau was finally at hand. The dedication ceremonies occurred at 10 a.m. on Sept. 11, 1898, and the Rev. Bishop Brondel of the

Cathedral of the Sacred Heart, of Helena, delivered a lecture in the evening.

Montanian publisher Corson mentioned the "liberal" Rev. Logan, this time, unlike Trescott, in a positive way. "In making his announcements last Sunday Rev. Logan said that in view of the fact that the Catholics had been so kind to himself and to his charge during the past four years, there would be no preaching at the M.E. church in the morning or evening. This he said is to enable all to attend the dedicatory services of the Catholic church in the morning and to attend Bishop Brondel's lecture in the evening. This is as it should be. 'Behold how good and how pleasant it is for brethren to dwell together in unity,'" Corson wrote.

On Sept. 16, Corson wrote a 1,200-word column on the dedication. He included his understanding of the history of the Catholic missions in the region, including the one near Priest Butte.

"Since the abandonment of the mission on the Teton in 1862, this section has passed from the territory of Nebraska to the state of Montana, out of the darkness of barbarism into the fullness of the light of the greatest civilization the world has ever known," he opined.

He said the bishop's service with the assistance of the Rev. Father Prando of Holy Family Mission from the reservation, lasted two hours and 20 minutes.

"On each side of the altar were a few beautiful plants and artificial flowers. Upon the altar itself were the necessary or usual articles only. Soon after the ceremonies were begun, the audience by request left their seats and passed outside and reverently awaited the bishop. In a moment he and the priest appeared and passing out, they turned to the left and slowly moved around the building followed by the congregation.

"As they moved, the bishop sprinkled the church with

Holy water, repeating at the same time the ritual service, the priest repeating the responses. Reentering the church and the audience being again seated, the inside was consecrated in like manner as was the outside, that is sprinkling the altar, the chancel and the walls with Holy water, and at the same time christening it St. Luke's church. ...

"In the evening the bishop lectured on the subject of the 'Holy Land' to an audience that filled every available seat in the church. Some were compelled to stand and many could not find standing room and so had to return to their homes. ... Bishop Brondel said he was pleased with Choteau, and with its people, and he warmly complimented his audience for its intelligence and good behavior," Corson wrote.

Brondel and Prando headed to the Blackfeet Reservation the next day, but not before Brondel "promised friends while he was here that he would endeavor to secure a priest for the Catholic church here as soon as possible," Corson said. He labeled the Rev. Prando as "one of the best men that ever lived. If all priests and preachers were as good, as unselfish and as energetic as he is, the kingdom of Satan would soon be curtailed if not destroyed."

A resident priest, however, was not immediately supplied. Catholic funeral services for Choteau's co-founder A.B. Hamilton's wife, Lucy, who died on March 2, 1899, were read by Mrs. Henri Beaupre, the local dentist's wife.

Then on April 21, 1899, the Montanian announced, "A letter received from Bishop Brondel by M.H. Ormsby the first of the week is to the effect that a priest has been sent here who will reside in Choteau and have charge of the work here as well as in Dupuyer and Augusta. This will be gratifying news to Catholics as well as to many others who have a kindly feeling toward people of that faith."

The Rev. Fr. Nicholas M. Snell celebrated his first Mass in Choteau on May 6, 1899, and his first Mass in Dupuyer on May 13, 1899. Born in Holland, Snell was 32 and had emigrated to the United States in 1896. His life story before coming to Montana is unknown.

In October 1898, the Dupuyer Acantha had mentioned that carpenters were working on the Catholic church there, but the Dec. 8 newspaper noted that work on the Church of the Holy Cross was stopped on account of the lack of funds.

However, the work continued under the guidance of Fr. Prando, a Jesuit priest based on the Blackfeet Reservation.

Acantha publisher Trescott wrote, "Father Prando has never tired in his efforts to push this undertaking along, traveling over sparsely settled sections of the country in all kinds of weather, in his earnest endeavors to raise money and assistance for the work he has voluntarily imposed upon himself. This revered gentleman has been connected with the Holy Family Mission, located on the Blackfeet Indian reservation about 24 miles north of Dupuyer, for some few years past, but has been on the frontier and among the Indians in Montana, engaged in his work as a priest for the past 18 or 20 years and is an earnest and sincere worker.

"Father Prando has used every economy in the building of this church here at Dupuyer and has taken the precaution to have it insured to as near its cash value as possible," Trescott wrote.

In January 1899 Prando was hospitalized at Columbus hospital in Great Falls, "as a result of over exertion and exposure to inclement weather," the Anaconda Standard said. On April 27, Prando announced to the Dupuyer faithful that henceforth, his entire time would be occupied with his work on the reservation. He was later transferred to St. Francis Xavier Mission on the Crow Indian Reservation. He died in the summer of 1906.

Before he left, however, Prando assured the Dupuyer faithful that Bishop Brondel would finish the construction of the church in Dupuyer, and once completed, a priest would be forthcoming from Helena. Snell was able to complete the church. Brondel died on Nov. 3, 1903.

Meanwhile, the rear room of the Catholic church in Choteau was being finished and furnished for use by Snell as a sacristy and library. A portion of it was made into a sleeping room.

Snell arrived from St. Peter's Mission in May 1899. "After saying Mass, Father Snell delivered a very interesting discourse on the subject of faith, and concluded the services with the sacrament of the Lord's Supper. Father Snell is a young man of fine presence, of decided oratorical abilities, and is a clear, logical reasoner. Not the least of his accomplishment is that of a musician, he being an exceptionally fine singer," Corson wrote.

Thereafter the newspapers announced his schedule each week and where he was headed next. Besides Choteau, Dupuyer and Augusta, he celebrated the Catholic sacraments in Shelby and Pondera, now known as Conrad, and Bynum. Snell was a busy man, traveling each Sunday to a different community to say Mass and administer the sacraments.

His base was a room attached to St. Luke's Catholic Church in Choteau. He celebrated Mass in the Dupuyer schoolhouse, but he told the Acantha editor that he expected to complete the Catholic church in Dupuyer during the coming summer.

The Montanian editor, who was very anti-Acantha, wrote, "He speaks well of the place and of the people and thinks the prospect is fairly good for success in his new field of labor there."

Being a musician, Snell and Mrs. J.E. Erickson were in charge of the music for Choteau's July 4th celebration.

He got a long write-up in the July 21, 1899, Montanian when he was involved in an accident. "Father Snell met with quite a mishap Monday afternoon at Chalmers' place on the Muddy on his return from Pondera. He was unhitching his horses in order to feed and rest them when one of them, made frantic by the flies and mosquitoes, began kicking and plunging, and in a moment both started on a run.

"So quick was their start that Father Snell could not get hold of the lines and away they went. The neck-yoke and tongue were soon broken and the team became detached from the carriage. Mounting a saddle horse, Father Snell pursued with perhaps somewhat less than Salvator speed.

"He had nearly caught up to them when they meekly turned around and walked back, meeting him in the most friendly manner. That was a remarkable circumstance, but then Father Snell is a Christian and these horses have been under the strictest kind of moral influence which perhaps accounts for the way they finally acted."

When the ladies of St. Luke's announced a benefit dance to be held at the town hall in Choteau on Sept. 8, Corson wrote, "Of course it will be a grand affair, for anything that the ladies of Choteau undertake to do is bound to be a success. Bear this in mind and remember the day and date." The event that included a cake walk raised $100.

In October Snell organized a Sunday school, and a choir after he secured an organ. He also hoped to have a children's choir in place, when the regular choir was not in attendance.

After that, Snell was frequently away from his flock going to Helena and elsewhere, even to the point of exasperation on Jan. 25, 1900, by Dupuyer's Trescott. "Where is the caretaker of the Catholic church? If the doors are not kept fastened, the building will be seriously damaged by the high winds which are now prevailing."

In June 1900, Snell announced that henceforth he would reside in Augusta, but he still ministered to the

Catholics in the other settlements, that now included Swift Current and St. Mary. His last official act in the Choteau area was to marry Florence St. Germaine and James Larance in November 1901 before he was transferred to the Belt parish east of Great Falls.

His priestly work continued until about March 1903, when a display ad in the Montanian announced the opening of the City Meat Market with N. Snell, proprietor; "Everything usually found in a first-class market."

Even more curious was the announcement a month later that Nicholas M. Snell, 34, and Pauline Muschek, 23, a divorcee, according to the marriage license, were quietly married at her residence in Choteau, by John E. DeHaas, justice of the peace.

"The bride was formerly from Belt and is an accomplished musician. The groom is a resident of Choteau, is engaged in the butcher business, and is well and favorably known in Teton County. The Montanian extends congratulations," Corson wrote.

Corson reported nothing of Snell's break with the church and no hint of scandal was noted when two months later, came a wedding announcement.

A census check showed Miss Muschek, 15, living in Belt in June 1900, with her parents. That record said Pauline was born in Austria in November 1884, so it would appear that she was only 18 when she married Nicholas. However, the marriage license filed in Teton County stated that she was 23, and divorced.

The couple set up residence in Choteau and Nicholas operated the meat market while continuing to participate in various musical activities, but then things began to unravel.

Pauline traveled to Belt for the birth of a daughter on March 16, 1904, but it appears she already had a daughter who was never mentioned before. At the same time

Nicholas sold the meat market to Severt Otness of Farmington. "Mr. Snell will probably remove to the coast," was all the Montanian said.

On July 14, 1904, the Choteau Acantha, which press had moved from Dupuyer the previous March, published the headline, "Ex-priest Snell sued for divorce," and the text spared no sympathy for the husband.

"Mrs. Pauline Helen Snell has filed with the Clerk of the District Court of Teton County a suit for divorce from her husband, Nicholas M. Snell. Mr. Snell is well known in northern Montana, having been a Catholic priest here for several years. He gave up the priesthood more than a year ago and was married in this city in June 1903, by Justice DeHaas.

"In her complaint the plaintiff alleges that there is now living of the issue of said marriage two minor children, May Pauline Snell, and Edna Helena Snell. That defendant by reason of his violent temper, idleness, profligacy and habitual intemperance is not a fit person to have the custody of the said children."

The article went on like that for four more paragraphs.

The Acantha did not end its righteous crusade with that. On Aug. 4, 1904, it published on the front page, "The last chapter of Nicholas." The article started with a verse, "A charming young priest named Snell, struck Choteau to save us from hell, but wine, song and jack-pots, out of Snell knocked the spots, and pell-mell he fell. Well! Well! What t'ell, Father Snell?

"The last chapter of Nicholas M. Snell's brief eventful and checkered career in northern Montana came to an end last Saturday at the special term of the district court held in Choteau by Judge Smith for the purpose of hearing the evidence in the divorce case brought by Mrs. Pauline Helen Snell. Upon the evidence of the plaintiff, the court awarded the decree of divorce, the defendant not making an appearance in court either in person or by attorney.

"Up to a few days ago, Snell declared his intention of fighting the case, but at the last minute was induced to accept a ticket to Montreal by parties connected with the church in Great Falls. He left that city last Thursday, and 'the old familiar haunts which once knew him will now know him no more forever.'"

The Acantha recapped Snell's history, ending with, "During his residence in Choteau, and while yet a priest, Snell conducted himself in a manner very unbecoming in a clergyman, and was reprimanded many times for his actions by the bishop."

Virtually tarred and feathered, Snell left town, and Pauline and her two children left a month later for Tacoma, Washington. The Acantha never mentioned the Snells again, but a check of the census reveals that by 1910, Nicholas, 42, still a butcher, and Pauline, 25, had reconciled and there was born a third daughter, Gladys, in the family.

It was not to last. Nicholas and Pauline were living apart in 1920, and the 1930 census lists him as divorced. Snell, 75, died in December 1943 and was buried in Calvary Cemetery in Tacoma.

18

Max Grotthuss, Russian Nobleman

May 25, 2016

It's not every community that can say it has a Russian nobleman as a resident, but for about 10 years during Choteau's pioneer days Baron Maximilian von Grotthuss called Choteau his home.

As with most celebrities, some news outlets repeated rumors of his exploits, but the local rags were more respectful in their remarks about Max when he died in April 1897 at age 38.

The Dupuyer Acantha wrote, "Baron Maximilian von Grotthuss is dead. For several weeks he has been an inmate of Dr. Drake's hospital in Choteau, and everything that could be done for his comfort was performed by his friends and his physician, but to no avail. Yesterday morning his earthly career was ended by death. Mr. Grotthuss had been a resident of this county for several years. A native of Russia, he was banished by the Czar, for political reasons, coming to New York City, where he met the Clark Bros., and with them came to Choteau."

The Montanian expanded on Max's life and his last illness, which appears to have started as the flu and then ended with pneumonia. His last name was spelled in at least four different ways in all the accounts.

"The deceased was a son of Baron Oscar von Grotthuss of Windau, Russia. He came to America some 10 years ago, and meeting with the Clark brothers, in New York, came to Choteau with them, and had been making his home with them until last fall, since which time he has made his home in Choteau in rooms secured at Dr. Drake's.

"About March 1, Grotthuss was taken seriously ill, gradually sinking away until his death, as above recorded, despite the truly eminent services of three noted physicians, Dr. Drake, Dr. Brooks, and Dr. Gordon, the latter coming up from Great Falls, and remaining with the sick man until his death. During his illness Grotthuss received several cablegrams from the Baron, his father, laying plans for his removal to his old Russian home as soon as he should be able to travel.

"Wednesday evening undertaker McBratney of Great Falls, arrived here with a costly casket and has embalmed the remains preparatory to their removal, but a cablegram today brings an order for burial here with simple prayers at the church and at the grave.

"Last year Grotthuss became a naturalized citizen of the United States and had taken land under land laws of the country, and otherwise exercised the privileges of an American citizen to show his good intentions, but as time has developed, all too late to avail him much profit.

"Max Grotthuss had some excellent virtues and many faults, but the latter concerned himself more than anyone else, and to them more than anything else is due his untimely death."

The New York Sun's April 19 edition had the most to say about Max's notoriety.

"He belonged to an old family in Russia, and when he left St. Petersburg in 1885, he was a lieutenant in the czar's guard. He was an inveterate gambler, fond of all kinds of sport, a favorite with men and the pet of women. His reputation was that he went a faster pace than any other man in his regiment. Debts accumulated. The allowance made him by his father was insufficient to meet his obligations. The father refused to increase the allowance and the young man came to America."

The Sun described his meeting the Clark brothers. "About the only thing the baron knew by which he could turn an honest penny was how to ride. He didn't care to follow the example of some of his countrymen in this country and turn riding master, so he applied to Walter Clark for a job on the ranch. Clark frankly told the baron that the only employment that could be had on the ranch was that of a sheepherder, whose pay was $40 a month. The baron agreed to take the job and went to Montana at once."

The Sun then described how Max would take his earnings and head to Helena once a year, where he would gamble them away, only to have Walter Clark settle his hotel bill before he left town. A week later, the Montanian wrote, "Somebody back in New York has been 'loading' the Sun with a lot of stuff about Grotthuss herding sheep," but the editor admitted that the one tale about Max's near shootout with a faro dealer was true.

About three months after the funeral, W.S. Clark went to the cemetery and photographed the grave. "This was done at the request of the deceased man's parents and relatives. They wished to have a view of the spot where the son and brother lies buried. Mr. Clark owns a Kodak and is an amateur photographer," the Montanian said.

19

Preacher's Kid to Movie Star

November 19, 2014

By the time the Rev. George Logan was appointed pastor of Choteau's Methodist Church in August 1894, his son, Frank, and his other four children were used to the family relocations that were a part of Logan's ministry in northern Montana.

The Choteau newspapers announced the family's arrival that August, and a month later reported on Pastor Logan's efforts to build, first a parsonage, and then a fine church in Choteau.

George and Margaret Logan's five children, Jessie, George E., Wilbur, Robert and Frank, seem to have assimilated well into Choteau's cultural circles, the news reports show. They did well in school, being "neither absent nor tardy," and gave recitals at the local literary society meetings. Robert and Frank were members of Choteau's juvenile cornet band.

Where Frank's acting bug bit him is unknown. In March 1899, Frank, then in eighth grade, was a cast member in a musicale and children's operetta at the Choteau town hall. Four months later he participated in the children's day exercises at the M.E. church which the local newspaper reported as "one of the finest entertainments of the kind ever given in Choteau."

Soon, however, the Rev. Logan reached the five-year limit of a minister's assignment and he was transferred to Sand Coulee. The family left behind, however, daughter

Jessie, who had married at age 18, and who died seven months later.

The Rev. Logan had a second pastorate in Choteau starting in 1907, but had to retire to Helena two years later. Meanwhile, son Wilbur had also died, a victim of typhoid fever while in Sand Coulee.

Frank's dramatic career, after graduating from Montana Wesleyan University, began on stage about 1915 in New York. The Acantha had a short blurb on his aspirations in June 1916. It said J. Frank Logan was a $150-a-week movie star who went by the stage name of J. Frank Glendon.

"The quality of his voice was such that he was induced to take up operatic work. For a number of years he was with the Mabel Page company as leading man, and made many successful tours in the east and south. About two years ago he went into the movie business," the news article said.

Movie historians note that Glendon moved to Hollywood and had starring roles in silent westerns and serial "cliffhangers." He took, most often, the part of the plot's handsome, often-mustachioed villain, the foil of heroes such as Gene Autry, Tim McCoy, John Wayne and others.

What's more, many of the movies were shown at the Royal Theatre in Choteau on Thursday and Friday each week. Rather than use a display advertisement, the promotion for a film was embedded in the local news column, for example, for this one titled, "For the Soul of Rafael," starring Clara Kimball Young.

"Have you ever pictured in your mind's eye a perfect motion picture, perfect in theme, plot, story, action, suspense and love element? Have you ever tried to visualize a photo drama so entrancing, so gripping and so highly entertaining as to walk miles if necessary to see it? ... We simply can't tell you the story. It's too splendid to try to tell in cold type. ... This is the one production of the season you must not miss, brought here at great expense. ... Frank Logan, a former Choteau boy, is the main support of Miss Young in this picture."

Frank had 82 films to his credit by the time he died in 1937. Not bad for a product of Choteau's schools. ▩

20

Sulgrove's Early History

July 17, 2013

Take any decade in Choteau's 130-year history (100 years as an incorporated town) and what is remembered and recalled for future generations is up to the storyteller.

Attorney James Sulgrove Sr. was just such a storyteller. He moved to Choteau in 1891 and was an authority on the county's history until he died in 1926. He played hopscotch with John E. Erickson, another Choteau attorney, in vying for the county attorney post in several early elections. Erickson would later become Montana's only three-term governor.

Sulgrove penned a timeline of significant events between 1904 and 1916 for the Oldest Settlers organization. The list made no mention of Choteau's incorporation on July 17, 1913, but it did include many "firsts" that shed light on the community's formative years.

The first automobile came to Choteau on April 9, 1904, driven by a man named Witten from Great Falls. Choteau hosted the first Teton County Fair in September 1906. The city got electric lights in July 1908 and the Great Northern railroad was completed to Choteau in September 1913. Before that, people had to ride the stage to the Collins train station 24 miles away in east-central Teton County.

A major fire destroyed the Bair building and other buildings in February 1905, and many others have been razed since then, but today's enduring symbol of prosperity and public service, the Teton County Courthouse, was completed in November 1906.

Another sign of prosperity and goodwill, the Episcopal (now Methodist) Church in Choteau was dedicated on Jan. 23, 1910.

The Acantha press, having been published in Dupuyer for 10 years, moved to Choteau and published the first Choteau Acantha edition on March 24, 1904, making it one of the oldest newspapers in the state in continuous operation.

Toole County was carved out of Teton County in May 1914, just as Teton County had been carved from Chouteau County in 1893. Pondera and Glacier counties followed, taken from Teton County in 1919. Teton County's extreme eastern section (east of a line between Brady and Power) was annexed during this period. The ensuing changes make up the county we know today.

A "great" hailstorm occurred on July 26, 1905, while a "big" hailstorm hit the city on June 25, 1915. Major floods occurred on June 5-7, 1908, and again on June 21-22, 1916.

Sulgrove said a record low temperature of -45 degrees occurred in Choteau on Jan. 26, 1916, but that never made it into the record books. Rather, the lowest January temperature that made the weather record was -44 on Jan. 24, 1943. The recordkeepers say that was the second lowest temperature ever recorded in Choteau, the first being a -50 reading on Feb. 15, 1936.

As to the highest ever temperatures, Sulgrove witnessed that too: 103 on July 20 and Aug. 3, 1893; 104 on Aug. 1 and Aug. 6, 1893; 105 on July 21 and Aug. 2, 1893, and on Aug. 25, 1894; and the whopper of all temperatures, 106 on Aug. 26, 1894. That makes the recent daily records of 95 and 96 on July 2-3, 2013, look tame in comparison, but still something to tell the grandkids about someday.

21

Ed Challenger, Escape Artist

Edward Challenger, some reports say his name was Edgar, had his debut in the world of crime on Aug. 12, 1904, when he allegedly broke into a Great Northern Railway Co. car near Conrad and stole several guns.

On Dec. 12 the Acantha reported that Sheriff C.W. Taylor left Choteau the first of the week for Chicago to bring Challenger back to Teton County for trial. Great Northern detectives went to work on the case and claimed at the time to have sufficient evidence to send Challenger "over the road for a long term."

His preliminary hearing was held on Jan. 10, 1905, before Justice J.E. DeHaas, where sufficient evidence was presented to bind him over to the district court in the sum of $1,000. Not being able to furnish the bail, he was remanded to the custody of the sheriff on a burglary charge and placed in the Teton County jail in Choteau.

He stayed in jail for a month. On March 6, 1905, a 12-man jury acquitted him.

However, immediately after Challenger's discharge, County Attorney Phil Cole filed a new "information," charging him with the crime of grand larceny for having stolen those same guns. Challenger was re-arrested and at once taken before the judge, who later ordered him released on his own recognizance.

After that, things began to unravel. In April 1905, Challenger pled guilty in Justice Evan Jones's court to the charge of assault with a deadly weapon in Conrad and was sentenced to six months in the county jail and fined $500, "which should keep him out of trouble for some time," the Acantha said.

A few days later came the news, "The first jail delivery [escape] for several years took place in Choteau last evening between eight and nine o'clock when Ed. Challenger and Geo. Odea [or Odes] made good their escape. A case knife was concealed by one of the prisoners and made into a saw, which was used to cut a bolt that secured the cell door.

"They climbed through a man hole to the roof of the jail, carrying a couple of blankets with them which they made fast to the chimney and lowered themselves to the ground," the Acantha reported.

On May 4, the Acantha reported, "Last week we reported that Ed. Challenger had broken out of jail. This week it becomes our duty to report that he has broken in again. After making his 'get-away,' he proceeded as far as Chester, in Chouteau County, where he fell in with a woman of the half-world with whom he was acquainted, and together they proceeded to paint the town a vermillion hue.

"John Barleycorn got the best of him and knocked him out, but not, however, until after his identity had been disclosed. Marshal Bickle of Havre went to Chester and woke Challenger with a natural — securely shackled hand and foot. Challenger was taken to Havre where he was turned over to Deputy Sheriff Daley of Shelby, who brought him back to his old home in our county jail. For some time, Challenger has been trying to break into the penitentiary, and it now looks as though he may succeed."

Having done it once, Challenger was out again within the month.

"During the past week, four prisoners have made their escape from the county jail at Choteau," the Acantha reported on June 1, 1905. The first to escape was awaiting trial for burglary.

Then on May 31, 1905, three more prisoners got away. During the temporary absence of the jailer, two prisoners, Joe Johnson and Linzy (or Linsy or Lindsay) Borst (or Lansing Berst), who were serving 60-day sentences for petit larceny, sawed the steel fastenings off the door leading from the cell room to the main entrance of the jail. They then broke into the jailer's office, where they secured the keys to the cells, and liberated Challenger. They then stole the guns and ammunition from the jailer's office and made their escape through the ventilator in the roof.

Sheriff Kenneth McKenzie, who had begun his term of office on Jan. 1, and Special Deputy S.C. Acton recaptured the men on the Teton River 40 miles northeast of Choteau.

The Havre Herald reported, "The trio made the mistake of traveling together and of stopping for the night with a herder in his hut on Bannatyne Bros.' ranch. The county surveyor of Teton County was encamped close by and readily recognized the fugitives. He immediately rode to Choteau and notified the sheriff, and the pursing posse was organized and trailed down the desperadoes with little difficulty."

Behind bars again, the men pled guilty to malicious mischief before District Judge Erickson. Challenger was sentenced to four years, Borst and Johnson to one year each, in the penitentiary in Deer Lodge. The Herald added that charges of grand larceny, burglary, and of having shot up the town of Dupuyer also hung over Challenger's head.

A mystery remains in that they are not listed as having been inmates in the Montana Prison Records available online. The Acantha never mentioned their names again.

22

Christmas 1906

December 26, 2018

Four Choteau businesses put half-page advertisements in the Choteau Acantha in December 1906 touting a variety of Christmas gifts for sale.

The Art Studio, owned by Thrya Haugen, dubbed her store the "Headquarters for Low Prices." A photographer by trade, Haugen offered courthouse and view calendars, photo frames at a 20-percent discount, candies, burnt leather novelties, 25 cents and up; handkerchiefs, three for 10 cents and up, and Mexican filigree and pyrites of iron jewelry, among other things.

The toy department sold wood carts, stick horses, kites, jump ropes, balloons, harmonicas, toy brooms, tea sets, pastry sets, toy whips, rubber balls, picture blocks, whistles, perfume, box paper, schoolboy pocket knives, pin cushions, toy books and children's pocket books, etc.

To encourage people to visit the store, Haugen raffled off a $6 leather pillow cover, one dozen $4 cabinets and a $3 framed study. Buyers earned tickets with every 50 cents' cash purchase.

The Jos. Hirshberg & Co. store with the logos, "We lead; let others follow," and "The big department store" ran an ad for "holiday goods galore."

"Every section of this big store is filled with holiday goods of all descriptions, new and seasonable merchandise. Christmas buyers will find it to their interest to inspect our holiday line that is full of quality, variety, beauty and good taste. We can please you as we have the right presents for everyone: old, middle-aged and young. Come in and see it and be convinced."

The ad continued, "Santa Claus is in the toy department and would be pleased to meet all the little folks. This is a remarkable treat for the children. Bring them in and let them see the toys such as mechanical clowns, doll houses, doll furniture, doll dresses, watches, merry-go-rounds, tool chests, sheep, hook ladders, clown acrobats, go-carts, pianos, doll tables, trunks, hobby horses, uniforms, washing machines, story books, loop the loop, doll dishes, children's desks, horns, games, trumpets, horses, ranges, guns, dolls, doll toilet sets, doll furniture, musical toys, automobiles, drums, bears, pipe organs and sail boats."

The ad for the City Drug Store, owned by Clarence Drake, enticed customers with a contest with four handsome dolls to be given away on Christmas Eve. "We will give to the most popular young lady in Teton County, her choice of four beautiful dolls, now on exhibition at our store, the result to be decided by vote. With each five cents cash purchase from now until Christmas you will be entitled to one vote. With each 10 cents purchase two votes, etc. The young lady receiving the next highest votes will have her choice of the remaining three dolls, etc."

The drug store sold books of poems, silverware, jewelry, Japanese china, games such as bridge, whist, flinch and zum zum, toys and trumpets, coffee mills, boy's sleighs, ladies and gents' sets and kids books, including Mother Wild Goose, Grimm's Fairy Tales, Rufus Rastus Brown, Katsenjammer Kids and Overall Boys.

The Choteau Mercantile Co. offered cut glass, china, silverware, candies and nuts, lemons, oranges, bananas and figs. Gifts for father included suit clothes, fur coats, Gordon hats, suspenders, mitts, pipes and buggy whips, while gifts for mother included table linen, rocking chairs, fancy table covers, handbags, corsets, overshoes, carving sets and carpet sweepers. Boys gifts included neckties, watch chains and skates and gifts for girls included fans, fancy combs, golf gloves, dress patterns, perfume boxes and Gunther's chocolates.

The store invited the "real Santa Claus" to visit on Dec. 24 for four hours and it promised a gift for each and everyone.

The Acantha reported a week later that Pearl Perman won first choice of dolls in the City Drug Store's contest with 7,280 votes. Nan Burrell, Hilda Monroe and Bernice Moore won the other dolls.

The newspaper also reported that the masquerade ball given under the auspices of the Choteau Baseball Club team at the Woodmen hall on Christmas night "was one of the most enjoyable affairs of the kind ever given in Choteau. There were 96 tickets sold and the boys cleared about $60 above expenses."

23

The Gem Restaurant

December 20, 27, 2017

Peter Joyce named his Choteau business the "Gem Restaurant," when it opened next door to St. Clair's barbershop in March 1894.

"Pete is an excellent 'chef' and knows exactly how to get up a good meal on short notice," the Montanian stated. Joyce advertised "chicken and ice cream after the dance" a month later.

The local newspapers, by all accounts, made much of a business opening, and served as boosters of all commerce in the city. They often mentioned when a business changed hands, but rarely mentioned when the same business that opened with so much promise quietly closed. Making a living running a restaurant had its challenges.

Joyce moved the Gem into new quarters in the Cooper building next door to Gibson and Walker's saloon the following year, but a year after that, came a new advertisement announcing that E.P. Butler relocated the Gem Restaurant into the Choteau House, a "first class hotel."

"Mr. and Mrs. Butler have conducted the Gem in such a way for some months past, that it has made them famous among epicures for the good things they provide at table, and we therefore have no hesitancy in recommending the Gem Restaurant and Choteau House as the proper place to stop at," the newspaper said in January 1896.

Two years later Joyce was back again after having searched for mineral wealth in the Ceded Strip. "Peter

Joyce, the proprietor of the new Gem Restaurant will serve the finest supper of the season to the dancers who attend the Republican rally on Friday night next," the Montanian said in October 1898.

The Teton Chronicle had more to say: "Peter Joyce opened up the Gem Restaurant in the St. Clair building today. He will run a first class house and solicits the public's patronage."

The new ad for the Gem read, "Best of service and attention to guests. Fresh bread, pies and cakes on sale at all times."

Joyce's active participation did not last. In June 1899 he sold the Gem to Ole Strand of Great Falls, although he may have done so on contract. Strand booked several wedding dinners during the following year that had a mention in the news. The Montanian said, "The supper given Wednesday night at the Gem Restaurant for the wedding dance is praised on all hands as one of the most elegant ever served in Choteau."

A month later in December 1899, the Gem changed hands again. "Charles E. Moore and [Oliver] 'Doc' Head have bought the Gem Restaurant of N.A. Strand and are now running the business. Mr. Strand will locate on the Burton Bench and engage in ranching." The pair did not last either.

In January 1900, Angus and Annie Bruce bought the Gem, probably buying Moore's contract that Joyce was carrying. "Mr. Bruce and his estimable wife have many friends in Choteau and vicinity and they will no doubt give satisfaction in the management of this popular restaurant. Doc Head will remain as chef which of itself will be a guarantee to the hungry public."

The Gem had its share of newsworthy events along with the menu ads. During a night in February 1900, "a cow belonging to T.J. Moore, while foraging for something good to eat or drink, got her head wedged in between the root house and ice house back of the Gem Restaurant and could not extricate herself. As soon as she was released in the morning she fell over dead from exhaustion and choking. She was a large fine animal and being a milch cow, her loss at this season of the year is quite serious," the Montanian wrote.

On July 4, 1900, the newspaper wrote, "When darkness fell upon the scene a grand display of fireworks was given at the intersection of Main and Conrad streets which was witnessed by several hundred people. As often happens on such occasions, there was a premature discharge of rockets, but fortunately they all went down toward Spring Creek grove and no one was hurt, though one of the blazing shafts went through a window of the Gem Restaurant and made free in a sort of friendly way with one of the waiter girls there."

The Gem catered the first Grand Concert given by the Choteau Brass Band at the town hall in March 1900, but few news bits appeared for a year.

Then a gala affair by the Chevalier Lodge No. 12 prompted the Teton Chronicle to publish the Gem's detailed menu for 20 "knights:" baked perch; roast chicken stuffed with robins with an Olympia oyster, rolled in browned cracker dust, on the inside of each robin; snails' tongues; celery, imported Waukesha water and Manila cigars."

In April 1901, Joyce finally sold all his interest in the Gem to the Bruces. He relocated to Pondera, now Conrad, where he was hired as the head chef in Mrs. Steele's hotel.

In August 1902, the Gem changed hands again, this time to Mrs. Ed. Dennis, but she soon gave it up to Soo Son, an immigrant from China who came to the area as a ranch cook for C. Wallace Taylor. Soo Son would become a fixture of Choteau's eating establishments along Main Avenue for the next 30 years.

The Gem Restaurant closed in April 1908, and Soo Son sold it to the Hirshberg brothers. They repurposed the building as a furniture store for a few months. They sold the building to Bert Stackhouse in May 1909. He had been the owner of the Club Café and when he moved to the new property, he renamed it the Stackhouse Restaurant.

Starting about 1913, ads for the Little Gem Restaurant appeared with A.O. Pond, proprietor. "Hot meals and short orders, open all hours day and night. Call in and see us. We can please you. First door north of Butcher Shop," the ads said.

Pond moved to a new location in J.E. Webb's former pool hall. In early 1914, he made the news: "A.O. Pond has entered on a 30-day fast in the hopes of reducing his flesh. He has gone 11 days including today, without eating any food and he proposes to keep up the fast until the end of 30 days.

"When he began the fast he weighed 310 pounds. He weighed himself today and found he had lost 26 pounds. He has tried all kinds of dieting and ransacked all the drug stores to reduce his fat. He has continually grown heavier until he was forced to take some drastic measure. He had hard work keeping awake while at work and would often fall asleep while standing on his feet. He says the week's fast has made him feel like a new man, and that he feels better than at any other time in the past two years. During all this 30 days fast, Mr. Pond expects to work every day waiting on his customers in the restaurant. He will drink water, but nothing else."

By Feb. 25, 1914, Pond had finished his fast and had lost 46 pounds. "He is eating lightly now and says that on Monday he will start on another fast, but for 40 days."

Nothing further was reported about his dieting. Pond expanded his business to open a new billiard hall next to the Little Gem, but six months later he lost interest and sold the Gem to J.W. Johnson.

In a confusing set of changes, Johnson apparently operated the Little Gem for a time, but by December 1914, the restaurant was turned into a shooting gallery on Main Avenue. "Special prizes will be made frequently for the best rifle shooting. Ladies are especially invited to become proficient in the handling of firearms," the Montanian stated.

Johnson sold the Little Gem building back to Pond in April 1915 and Pond ran it as an eatery until May 1917 when he sold it to Roy Milton and R.C. Wood of Seattle. They changed the name to the Merchant's Lunch, later the Merchants Café. Their ad read, "Open day and night. Hot meals and short orders. We employ the highest salaried cooks in Teton County, which means better meals, better service and more for your money. A trial will convince." The Gem name was no more after that, but other restaurants, including Soo Son's took its place.

24

Citizens State Bank turns 100

July 22, 2009

A report that a new bank was going to open in Choteau made the front page of the Choteau Acantha in February 1909, and that one modest article marked the beginning of the Citizens State Bank of Choteau that celebrated its centennial in July 2009.

As it happens, the news item erred in naming the new institution the "National Bank of Choteau," but Acantha publisher A.B. Guthrie Sr. corrected the bank's name in the edition published two weeks later.

The new bank was the second one in town, providing choice for the community and a competition between Citizens State Bank and the bank that the Hirshberg brothers had organized in 1902. The competition continued until the Hirshbergs' bank, later called the First National Bank of Choteau, closed in 1934. (The Antler Bar is now located on the site of the Hirshberg bank.)

Citizens State Bank was the third bank to operate in Choteau. An earlier Bank of Choteau opened in 1892, but it closed in the economic panic of 1893.

Rancher George M. Coffey Sr. (1866-1928) and Helena banker James Eckford (1880-1930) organized Citizens State Bank on March 4, 1909, with a capital stock of $50,000.

The bank opening did not go off without a hitch as the men remodeled their new quarters on upper Main Avenue and added bank furniture. The directors set up business in the Hodgskiss building that had formerly been used as the Teton County courthouse until the new courthouse opened in 1906.

The Acantha reported that the men encountered "considerable trouble" because the combination to the Hodgskiss building's old vault was lost.

"The old vault has defeated all attempts made to open it," the newspaper said. No one knows for sure, but Clerk of District Court Sterling McDonald must have come to the rescue. He was the last one to use the vault.

Soon the bank had resources of $75,000 and a 1913 advertisement offered "the advantage of its facilities developed and perfected by close personal relationship with a constantly growing list of depositors."

Two years later the bank moved to the newly built Larson Block, and into the ground-floor corner suite where Choteau Drug is now located. At the same time, the bank ran a new display advertisement that stood out from the normally tightly-spaced type in the Acantha.

"Personality" in big bold letters, the ad read, "in business is equally as important as stability. We believe that courtesy is a valuable asset to any institution, and this we offer you, coupled with safe, sane and conservative financial practice. Your account is invited."

Business was good, so good that a new set of investors decided to set up Stockmens State Bank on April 5, 1919, the fourth bank to open in Choteau, with Sterling McDonald's son, Charles S. McDonald, as president and with director Fred Woehner and others. Their plans included a new building to house their business.

From pioneer Choteau businessman William Hodgskiss, they purchased the site of the old Silverman & Cohen store at the corner of Main Avenue and Second Street, regarded as "one of the best business locations in the city."

They razed the old store and constructed the new bank in short order.

It was not long, however, before the competition between banks for a decreasing number of customers had changed the business climate in Choteau. On July 14, 1927, the Acantha announced that Stockmens and Citizens had merged in a deal to consolidate banking operations under new management, but keeping the name, Citizens State Bank.

The staff included C. Denzel McDonald (1896-1950), former cashier of Stockmens, who became assistant cashier at Citizens.

A new face also appeared in the banking community at this time. Great Falls banker Fred Barribal (1903-1985) had worked for a short time at Citizens in 1927, but took the job permanently in 1928.

Citizens State Bank and the other banks survived the Crash of 1929 as the nation's economy deteriorated. President Franklin Roosevelt declared a "bank holiday" on March 5, 1933, for four days to save the nation's banks from a run on their cash reserves and to implement new legislation regulating banks.

All Teton County banks opened on March 15, 1933 for regular business under the new rules that prohibited the withdrawal of gold in any form or of gold certificates. Currency could not be withdrawn for hoarding, and if a bank permitted it, the bank and the hoarder could each be subject to a $10,000 fine.

The county's banks included the First National and the Citizens State at Choteau, the First National at Fairfield, Dutton State at Dutton, First State at Bynum, Power State at Power and Farmers State at Pendroy. However, some of them closed in a few years' time. (A bank in Bole located between Fairfield and Choteau had already closed in 1920.)

Peter Bouma, 84, who was born in Bole on the Teton Ridge, related a family story that shows the power that the banks had over peoples' lives.

"My parents, Louie and Nina Bouma, moved back from South Dakota in 1933. Dad knew Ed Hirshberg [the bank manager of the First National Bank of Choteau] and met him on the street. Before the conversation was over, Dad had a farm to move to," Bouma said.

Retired banker George Higgins, 76, who lives on a ranch south of Choteau, said that before the banks could open, they had to prove they were solvent. He said Citizens cashier Barribal and Denzel McDonald, by now a vice president at Citizens, personally went to Helena taking with them a $5,000 U.S. government bond to be used as security so that Citizens State Bank could re-open.

As the tough times continued, the bank directors sought other cost-savings measures. They decided to move from their rented space in the Larson building to the old Stockmens building that they owned but that had been vacant since 1927. The move occurred about the same time that Barribal bought out Woehner's interest in the bank in 1938, becoming a bank partner with Denzel McDonald.

The bank served the community during the war years and when the war was over, Dorothy Armstrong, a married 21-year-old Choteau graduate, got a job there.

Armstrong, 85 in 2009, cheerfully reminisced about her time at the bank in a phone interview from her home in Kennewick, Washington, she shared with her son, Scott. She retired at age 65 in July 1989, having worked at Citizens for her entire career except for four years when Scott was born.

She started as a teller on Jan. 2, 1946.

Armstrong said every check was reviewed by hand. "We had to know what wife matched what name and who was on the accounts," she said, noting that she was the third female to work there. Armstrong took the place of Irene Talifson who with Dorothy O'Neil were the first women to work there. The bosses referred to them as "Dorothy A." and "Dorothy O."

Armstrong said that Teton County High School boys, Bob Gronberg and Charles "Buddy" Hallberg, a popular basketball player, were Barribal's and McDonald's picks, respectively, to be trained as bank officers. They were in the class of 1938.

Both young men were in the service, but Hallberg, a fighter pilot, died in France in 1944. Gronberg returned to take his place in the bank.

"Bob was Fred's choice to be groomed to climb the ladder to success. Girls could not go very far," Armstrong said. "We girls got to be assistant cashier, the highest title we could get."

The year 1950 contained two vivid memories for Armstrong. On Sunday, Sept. 18, 1950, McDonald died unexpectedly of a heart attack.

"I remember that Fred asked us to come in early. We were shocked and waited on customers with tears in our eyes," Armstrong said. In the aftermath, Barribal acquired McDonald's interest in the bank and became its president.

She began the second story by saying that the bank was the first business to have a Santa Claus come in at Christmas time to give candy to the kids under a decorated tree.

It had been a very cold winter. Out on the sidewalk the metal grates to the old coal bin were covered with ice. No longer used for coal deliveries, the room below the sidewalk was used to store the bank's Christmas stuff.

An investigation determined later that the ice prevented the coal bin from venting and at some point a gas leak had developed in the little room. Outside the room in the basement stood a big gas furnace and a gas-fired water heater.

On Dec. 27, 1950, Barribal went downstairs to put the Christmas decorations away. As soon as he opened the storage room door, leaking gas from the broken line ignited in a huge explosion that sent a shockwave through the basement and up the stairway, which an employee had just left.

"Connie Kuster and I were sitting on stools sorting checks. I felt a pressure, and saw Connie bend down to the floor. I followed her. In that instant, the clock flew by and hit the window behind us. All the windows were blown out and glass covered the sidewalk," Armstrong said.

"Fred came up the stairs hollering with his shoes and jacket on fire. When I pulled off his jacket, his skin came with it. Joe Knudtzon and Carl Wedum were nearby and I yelled to get an ambulance. A fire siren blew and it was a wonderful sound," Armstrong said.

She suffered two broken eardrums from the blast and Barribal had a long recovery to heal the burns.

Checks went everywhere, in the chandeliers and out on the street, she said.

Within hours, Knudtzon, who owned a lumberyard in town, boarded up the windows and the girls worked in the unheated, darkened bank with their coats on, until they found all the checks and balanced the books.

During Armstrong's time out to have a child, Higgins joined the staff at the bank. He had just finished a stint in the army when Barribal offered him a job for $200 per month.

The pay was less than he had received driving a county truck at $340 per month before he was drafted in 1953.

Armstrong, who returned to work in 1959, said the bank was never robbed, however, thieves "cased" the bank once. "Our money was in the little safe in the vault. There was a pistol and a holster right inside the vault door, and a rifle or a shotgun, by our coats. If we were robbed, I guess we were supposed to use them," she said.

She said that after a robbery at the bank in Valier, Barribal announced, "No one is going to risk their life for this money," and he removed the guns and put in an air vent in the vault, so the employees would have fresh air, if they were forced in there. The vault was on a time lock and Armstrong was the one who opened the vault in the morning.

In 1965 Barribal sold his stock to Gronberg, who had been a bank director since 1951. Higgins recalled that Gronberg got the extra money he needed for the buyout by setting up a partnership with John Brandvold of Great Falls, a man he hardly knew.

"I was the peacemaker between the two," Higgins said.

In 1970, Gronberg and his wife began to spend time as snowbirds in Arizona and Higgins ran the bank while he was away. Starting as a teller Higgins was promoted over the years to bookkeeper, assistant cashier, cashier, vice president and director and, finally, vice president and executive officer.

Jennie Bouma Garramon of Choteau worked at the bank from 1972 to 1977 as a general bookkeeper.

"We were one of the few banks, if not the only bank in the state, that had Saturday hours. We took turns bringing lunch. The smell of the good food carried through the building," she said.

"The first time I ever stepped in a bar was to try to collect on bum checks," she said, laughing.

The sale of Citizens State Bank in November 1982 was front-page news. Higgins said Gronberg bought out Brandvold's interest within hours of selling the bank to brothers Duane S. "Duke" Amundson from Plentywood and Lloyd A. Amundson from Sioux Falls, South Dakota, along with a group of investors.

Higgins continued to manage the bank but a new chapter had begun. The Amundsons erected a new building across the street from the old location, razing the old buildings housing the Pioneer Bar and Ear Mountain Machinery in the process. Zion Construction was the contractor. The bank went from 2,000 square feet to 6,000 square feet.

Citizens opened in its new home on Oct. 26, 1984, which coincided with the bank's 75th anniversary. More than 1,100 people attended the event.

Armstrong, who was an assistant cashier when the Amundsons bought the bank, recalled an incident with the new owners that got "her nose out of joint." She said, "I handled all the money and when Lloyd saw the amount of money I had, he told me, 'That is not good money management.' I knew what I was doing, I had pipeline crews in there," she said, explaining the necessity for having lots of cash.

Higgins also noticed a change in bank operations. He said the new owners set up a loan-servicing committee that resulted in a reduction in the number of loans granted. The owners cashed in some high-interest government securities, assets that the former owners had put together over five years.

Duke Amundson in May 1986 turned the bank management over to his son, Mike, and after 31 years at Citizens, Higgins was out.

The Citizens State Bank made front-page news again on May 11, 1989, when Mike Johnson of the First National Bank of Fairfield announced to the Choteau Chamber of Commerce that his family, through a family-owned holding company, had begun the lengthy process to purchase Citizens.

The First National Bank of Fairfield had been under common ownership for four generations after FNB bank manager John Young, Johnson's great-grandfather, bought out Ed Hirshberg's interest in the bank that the Hirshberg brothers had organized in 1919.

"The Fairfield family buying Citizens State Bank was one of the best things to happen to Choteau," Higgins said.

Both Armstrong and Higgins and many long-time former employees have numerous stories of their banking days, but the latest chapter is being written by the bank's dozen employees, such as assistant cashier Lorry Rasmussen, who has worked at the bank for 23 years.

In an interview in July 2009, FNB President Johnson said, "We are thankful that we are a community bank focused on serving a small fairly-remote geographic area given the crisis in the current economy. We don't know anything but community banking, and we don't want to know. It's a simple conservative philosophy that is serving us better than it ever has."

He continued, "We don't own those banks, the community does. We need their deposits to make loans to create the tax base and be the conduit that supports the community."

He invited the community to the centennial celebration at the bank from 4 p.m. to 7 p.m. on July 23, 2009, with a family barbecue, live music, refreshments, prizes, gifts and fun for the whole family.

In various transitions since that time, the family-owned Teton Bancshares Inc., which operated the Citizens bank in Choteau and one in Fairfield, merged with Intermountain Bancorp Inc. of Bozeman (First Security Bank.) In March 2018 Intermountain Bancorp merged with the Glacier Bancorp family of banks. The name of the longtime Choteau bank changed to First Bank of Montana, a division of Glacier Bank.

— 25 —

Slogans

October 10, 17, 24, 2018

People have used slogans for everything from selling their goods and services to selling themselves during elections; and newspapers, with their desire for brevity, have embraced them all.

For example, the "Made in America" slogan first appeared in the Montanian in December 1914. The slogan was "receiving considerable impetus by the trade papers more particularly and by the daily press more or less all over the country. It seems an excellent opportunity to put over something that will be of great benefit to the manufacturers of this country and, of course, anything that benefits them in a large way is bound to benefit the workmen and, incidentally, the general prosperity of this country."

The state Chamber of Commerce staged a three-month campaign starting in October 1921 with the cumbersome slogan, "Price and quality being equal, Montana-made goods should be used in Montana in preference to all others." Wisely, they shortened that to "Made in Montana" by December. "It will be a month devoted to carrying into every Montana home and store, a message of state patriotism," the Acantha noted.

The latter phrase persisted into modern times, but some others did not. The Montana Federation of Woman's Clubs debuted, "Montana products for Montana people," in 1924, which soon faded away.

Catch phrases showed up in advertisements for local

businesses as soon as Choteau got a newspaper. The Choteau House in 1891 was a "first class stopping place for everybody." By 1950, the Choteau House Bar and Lounge had changed that to, "You're never a stranger in the Choteau House but once."

The Choteau Mercantile Co. had three slogans: "Quality and Service" in 1917, while promoting the Great Majestic Range, a stove; and in 1920, it used "The big store with the little prices" and "We sell for less" in its ads. Also in 1920, J.W. Oppie's ad for the Beaupre Café announced, "The Best Meals in the State for the Money."

The Fashion Tailor Shop in 1915 proclaimed, "We clean clothes clean," while the long-running establishment, the Jos. Hirshberg & Co. store, in 1931 used these words, "Before sending away to mail order houses, try us first. Our slogan is 'We must sell it for less.'" It sold everything from Hart Schaffner and Marx clothes to furniture, hardware and groceries.

Choteau saloonkeeper Alex Longmuir in 1934 used the slogan, "The second bottle from the window," whatever that meant. The Choteau Acantha began using the slogan, "Published Once a Week; Read Every Day," on Jan. 19, 1950, when co-editors Jere Coffey and Pat Campbell operated the newspaper. That slogan has lasted 68 years and counting.

Organizations often used slogans. When the Young Women's Christian Association launched the Girl Reserves in 1918, the slogan was, "To Face Life Squarely." The Choteau 4-H club in 1936 used the phrase, "Make the better best."

Every manner of celebration or event had its own slogan. In September 1936 "Come and Get it" was the slogan commemorating the completion of the Lewis and Clark highway (route 33, now U.S. Highway 287), which was the section between Augusta and Choteau. The party was at the

American Legion pavilion in Choteau, with places set for 315 guests, free music, food and beer. Lou Brodecker, chief of the Montana Highway Patrol, promised to pilot the Helena gang into Choteau, but the Acantha added, "He will not assume any responsibility for getting them home."

The Highway Patrol produced a slogan each spring before the tourist season, although they tended to be a bit long like this one from 1939, "If you wish to be alive tomorrow, be careful today."

Mrs. Charles McCarthy of Fairfield submitted the winning slogan to the 1961 Safety Slogan contest, aired by KMON in Great Falls. Her slogan was, "What we need for the modern car, are drivers as good as they think they are!"

Choteau's July 4th celebration always had a theme or slogan, during the days when the Choteau Lions Club hosted it and later when the Choteau Chamber of Commerce coordinated the event. "A big time for little money," was selected for 1938.

The Lions in November 1928 decided, "This growing city needs a slogan or a nickname, if you please, that will rebound to its glory in the outside world. Montana is the Treasure State; Great Falls, the Electric City; Missoula, the Garden City; and Choteau is — well what? That's the question."

So the Lions proposed to find out and appointed a committee to formulate some plans along the line of arranging for a contest in which prizes would be awarded for the best slogan. The committee members, the Rev. E.R. Kaemmer, E.L.Jourdonnais and W.E. Lockhart, met and mapped out a plan.

By November they had set the rules and prizes, a $10 first prize and a $5 second prize for the best slogan typifying Choteau. The deadline was Dec. 10.

Any person living in Teton County was eligible to

compete by submitting a slogan not to exceed four or five words, and the shorter the better. The Lions asked teachers to interest school children and in case of duplications, the first received would be given preference. The club reserved the right to reject all slogans in case no suitable slogans were received.

"What the club wants is a short snappy expression which in a certain sense characterizes the town. For instance, Miles City is Cow Town, Minot is, 'Why not Minot?', Portland is the Rose City, Bozeman is Sweet Pea City, etc."

The Lions proposed that the judges would be representative persons of the community who were well fitted to render a fair and impartial decision.

On Nov. 15, the Acantha reported that the committee was "anxious to get many more suggestions. So wake up folks and get busy! There's fame as well as fortune if you win, and besides, you will do the town and the community good if you name a slogan which has pep and which aids in expressing the ideals and aspirations of the community."

A reminder on Nov. 22, added, "Develop a slogan which may be flung far and wide to the profit and honor of Choteau. Pride in one's place of residence is a birthright that every American citizen can express with certainty. Pride is not to be confounded with vanity. The latter detracts; it rides to a fall. Pride is constructive, it is progressive; it builds."

The Lions suggested that the city could erect a sign of welcome similar to the one at the entrance to Great Falls. "And back it up by extending a smile, a hand shake and a cheery greeting to the worthy stranger who comes in our midst. It's good business to do so and it's humanity."

As the Dec. 10 deadline neared, the committee had only 67 slogans to choose from so it extended the deadline to Jan. 10, 1929. "Due to the large amount of sickness, it was thought that many would send in slogans if the time were extended who have hitherto been unable," the Acantha reported while noting the high number of people who had contracted flu.

The Acantha published one more reminder on Dec. 27 to "Get your slogans in now that Christmas is over and the holiday vacation is at hand. The slogan committee desires to again call attention to the contest deadline, Jan. 10."

The Lions Club never announced who the judges were, but on Feb. 14, 1929, the Acantha published the winning entries.

"Out of about 150 slogans submitted in the slogan contest, that submitted by Mrs. C.H. Porter was selected for the $10 prize by the club in session Wednesday evening. R.E. Nelson submitted the slogan, which was awarded second prize.

"Mrs. Porter's slogan was, 'You'll like Choteau,' and Nelson's was, 'Where the hand clasp is stronger.' Neither of the slogans were officially adopted by the club," the Acantha reported.

Note that Nelson's slogan was six words long, in violation of one of the contest rules. One wonders what went on at that club meeting to bring about a consensus in choosing the underwhelming selections, which never appeared in any subsequent Acantha editions.

As the years went by, the state changed its slogan from "The Treasure State" to the "Big Sky Country," thanks to author A.B. "Bud" Guthrie Jr., and Choteau would eventually become the "Gateway to the Rocky Mountain Front."

The Choteau IGA Super Saver grocery store used a similar phrase starting on Dec. 21, 1989, when the logo, "Choteau, Gateway to the Rockies," appeared in the store's large weekly Acantha ad.

Storeowners Wayne Morris and Rick St. Onge held a grand opening earlier in February after they bought the store from Gary Durocher.

The Super Saver celebrated its one-year anniversary on Dec. 21 with the new logo, a line drawing of a mountain skyline and the words, "Choteau, Gateway to the Rockies."

The store went out of business in May 1990, and it was not until May 11, 1994, that the phrase "Gateway to the Rocky Mountain Front," appeared for the first time in the Acantha, although one figures city residents knew the phrase.

The Montana Specialties shop ad read, "For lasting memories, order your Gateway to the Rocky Mountain Front cotton throw blanket today. Specially designed and personalized for this area. Special price for early orders."

Ottis and Sylvia Bryan operated Montana Specialties at 38 Main N. at the time, using the shop slogan, "For graceful living and thoughtful giving."

Their May 25 display ad for the cotton throw read, "Limited first edition, $45; $50 after June 3; depicts the scenery, wildlife, industry and people of this area." A design of livestock brands ringed the throw along with the "Gateway" slogan.

In a December 1999 interview, Lyall Stott, the father of Eagle Scout Travis Stott, credited his son with a project to erect the first sign at the entrance of town announcing the city's motto, "Gateway to the Rocky Mountain Front."

Around April 2006, the Choteau Chamber of Commerce began using the "Gateway" slogan for its promotional material. In 2013 the old "Gateway" signs were replaced with metal signs with a new phrase, "Welcome to Choteau, in the valley of the Teton."

A search of the old news shows that the first mention of Choteau being the "Gateway to the Rockies," was a long Acantha article published on June 29, 1933, without a byline. Ernest L.Jourdonnais was the owner and publisher at the time.

The article began, "Vacationland. 'Home on the range, where deer and antelope play.' If you would see in reality what this famous western ballad tells, if you would recreate in the great outdoors of the west, if you would bag an elk, trail a bear or land a rainbow, then follow the trails that lead to Teton and Choteau — Gateway to the Rockies."

Starting with antelope, the article explained, "Teton County is one of the few counties of the West where one may still see the antelope in their native habitat. The buffalo are gone, and the elk, once a native of the plains, have taken refuge in the rugged hills and high mountains. But a few antelope remain and the sight of them is worth driving over half a continent.

"Indeed, men do travel that far to see buffalo, and then only to be greeted with the knowledge that reserves have been created for them and they are in only a semi-wild state.

"Not so with our antelope. They have withstood all the advances of civilization. Their ranges have been fenced and their pasture turned to domestic hay or wheat, but they have refused to go and their persistency has made them friends. The law protects them, and this is backed by a strong public sentiment. Woe to the poacher if he is caught!"

The writer claimed that about 100 antelope lived in the county in two main bands. One frequented the regions south of Choteau and west of Fairfield, and grazed most generally on the Pat Crossen, H.E. Knust, Jasper Murray, Nick Vlinker, Vincent Vance and Martin Rose ranches.

"Travelers between Choteau and Augusta are likely to see them any time when they reach the top of the bench on the road that leads out of the Deep Creek valley," the article stated. The second band ranged east of Fairfield and south of Power with as many as 60 counted on the Jerry Kelleher and Alvin Johnson ranches in that locality.

— 26 —

Boom Town Scrapbook

November 23, 2005

A scrapbook of newspaper clippings from the early 1900s offers a glimpse of life in Choteau, thanks to New York resident Daniel Haley.

Haley sent his father's scrapbook to the Acantha in October 2005. "I hope you will be able to make up several good stories from it," Haley wrote in his cover letter.

In 1914, the Rev. Leon F. Haley was the Episcopal minister for Teton County. He lived in Choteau and preached there and in Conrad and Valier. He supplemented his income by being a special correspondent to the Daily Tribune in Great Falls. He saved his columns, now yellowed with age, in a tattered scrapbook that his son, Daniel, of Waddington, New York, found in the summer.

Rev. Haley left Choteau around 1920 to take a parish in Cleveland, Ohio, and to be nearer to his aging parents. His son recently sold the ranch in Teton County that his father homesteaded in 1914.

The minister's columns, which ran from October 1913 to October 1914, offer a snapshot of life in Choteau during a time of expanding population and commerce. Choteau had been a settlement since 1883, but its future was secured when townsfolk incorporated the city in May 1913.

Haley's articles begin with a note on a snowstorm. Two feet of snow fell over a weekend in October 1913, and all commerce involving travel had stopped. Salesmen, holed up in the Choteau hotels, played chess while they waited for the roads to be passable again. At the same time, more than half of the children in the grade school were out sick with measles.

The Great Northern Railway announced that it would build a 90-foot-long freight and passenger station in Choteau while it was completing its Power-Choteau-Bynum route.

In 1913 Choteau began to build a new water and sewer system. The city agreed to lay sidewalks around town, but it had not yet improved the unpaved, gravel streets that were impassable during especially wet weather.

During hunting season, Haley plugged the town, saying, "Choteau is the gateway to the best hunting grounds in the west. With proper advertising, it could be made as famous as Cody, Wyoming."

On Nov. 11, 1913, the railroad arrived in Bynum with much celebration. "Today it promises to become a little Chicago, so great are the hopes of its citizens," he said, noting that the school had 40 children enrolled.

That fall several grain elevators were built and the first grain arrived at the depot in November for shipment on the new railroad.

In February 1914, the stage could not bring the mail to town via the 25-mile overland route from the Collins railroad depot. "On account of the raw wind that raked over the prairie all day Wednesday, the stage did not leave the barn," Haley wrote, adding that it would be a happy day for Choteau "when the stage coach days are torn off the calendar."

His wish came true when on Feb. 16, 1914, the mail arrived on a passenger train for the first time.

Old timers noted that two or three feet of snow should be found at the Sun River Hot Springs, but in early 1914, the ground was almost bare.

Haley wrote, "There is considerable snow farther up on the high ridges along the Continental Divide, but what is needed, the old timers say, is a heavy snow fall and then a good thaw and then more snow, so that ice will be formed all over the hillsides. This is the way nature generally stores water for the entire season."

Reports of new homes and commercial buildings peppered Haley's columns. He noted that architect George H. Shanley of Great Falls planned the new $3,000 façade for the Joseph Hirshberg & Co.'s store. The new front "will be entirely modern and strictly up to date," he said.

The region had its share of murder and mayhem in 1914.

William "Tex" Smith was found murdered near Priest Butte Lake, apparently killed for the $250 he had in his pockets.

Dr. C.W. Dawe went on trial at the courthouse in Choteau charged with first-degree murder for killing Charlie "Chapparall" Clifford of Valier.

Dawe's family said he was crazed with drugs and alcohol at the time. During the trial, Dawe's mother "went into hysterics and had to be carried bodily from the courtroom." Defense attorney Logan's summation lasted two hours, and according to Haley, "Mr. Logan was listened to with rapt attention." The jury convicted Dawe of manslaughter in a compromise verdict, because some of them thought he was insane.

While Dawe's jury was still wrangling over the verdict, Judge H.H. Ewing empaneled a new jury in the trial of James Johnson, who was charged with murder for killing a man named Jackson at Cut Bank.

Johnson was found guilty and both Dawe and Johnson were sent to prison in Deer Lodge for 10 years.

In August 1914, Haley reported that a forest fire was raging between McDowell and Rock creeks and that it had expanded to be 10 miles long. Two special trains with more than 100 men came up from Great Falls and unloaded men who were driven to the mountains where they had to walk 20 miles to the fire. The Forest Service paid the locals $20 per car to take the men to the Ear Mountain Ranger Station and several residents made four or five trips.

Haley used his columns to write about his ministry. In an October 1914 column, he wrote, "We are all proud of our town, and hope to see it advance rapidly toward a more modern and up-to-date city. Why not begin with the first Sunday in November, next Sunday, and encourage your ministers by filling their pews. Churchgoing is a habit, and a very good habit to get into. It's better to form the habit of churchgoing than to remain in the bad habit of sleeping till noon."

In one of his last columns in the scrapbook, Haley wrote, "The weather for the past few days has been so delicious to the taste that nearly everybody is wearing the Montana smile that makes us feel proud to live in the 'Treasure State.'

"Farmers are bringing their grain in double wagon box loads to the elevators. Others are either plowing or sowing their winter wheat. Homesteaders are all feeling happy over the bright outlook of another season, and merchants are enjoying a very prosperous business. One day this week over 20 teams were counted hitched up to the posts back of Hirshberg Bros.' store. Nearly as many more were lined up in front of Strain Bros.' store or at other places along the street."

He added, "Kirt Grunwald, vice president of the International Irrigation Congress, of Denver, Colorado, has been looking over the agricultural possibilities around Choteau. He has in mind a sugar beet factory for this locality. He was very enthusiastic in his praise for this valley. He predicted a very bright future for Choteau."

— 27 —
Annie Laurie Bruce
December 13, 2017

Angus Bruce and Annie Laurie Elliott reckoned it was a good omen when they saw a meteor falling in the Sun River Canyon on Sept. 17, 1897.

Three months later on Dec. 29, Annie, 22, married Angus, 37, the wedding being one of Choteau's social events of the season with 60 guests in attendance.

The Montanian wrote about the gala affair, ending with this snippet: "Angus Bruce has been known by his friends as a man with the strength of an ox, the agility of a panther, the courage of a game cock, and as one possessing nerve enough to refrain from coughing with a fish bone lodged crossways in his throat, but when it became necessary for Angus to repeat the marriage vows — well, most any of the boys could have talked equally as well."

They both hailed from Canada, Angus arriving first in Fort Benton and Great Falls before settling in Choteau in the fall of 1891. He and his brother William became American citizens in September 1892.

Annie came to Choteau in 1895 to visit her sister who was married to William. She stayed, having been introduced to William's handsome bachelor brother who had a homestead and stock ranch west of Choteau. After the wedding, the couple moved to town and rented rooms in James Gibson's residence.

In a series of business enterprises, some successful and some not so much, Angus bought a feed and livery business, opened a meat market and went into the saloon business. With the news that the state Legislature had created Teton County in March 1893, he moved the business into new quarters and renamed the bar, the "New County Saloon and Club Rooms." He sold that in November 1894.

In 1899 he and a partner started a line of express and passenger coaches daily between Choteau and Steell station on the Great Falls & Canada Railway, a location southeast of Freezout Lake.

The couple bought the Gem Restaurant in 1900 but sold it in August 1902 after Angus had a series of illnesses. They traveled after that and their names were seldom in the newspapers. Angus worked on occasion for Teton County over the years, serving as the Choteau road district supervisor and as a court bailiff.

They sold their 674-acre ranch in September 1916, and spent the winter in California. They came back to Choteau the following summer and were enjoying a quiet fall evening at their Main Avenue residence on Sept. 7, 1917. The Acantha and other newspapers reported what happened next.

Annie was filling a Rochester lamp with kerosene while the wick was lighted when it exploded. Angus was reading in an adjoining room, and, as his wife rushed toward him enveloped with flames, he threw rugs about her and did everything possible to extinguish the flames. But it was not until people on the porch of the Glenloyd hotel across the street rushed to the Bruce home and carried her out on to the lawn that they were successful in putting out the fire.

"Mr. Bruce was considerably burned about his hands, but was otherwise uninjured. Mrs. Bruce, however, was literally roasted from her head to her feet," the Montanian reported. She was rushed to McGregor Bros. hospital in an auto, where everything possible was done to relieve her sufferings, but in spite of this, death from shock ended it all at 7:30 the following morning. She was 42.

"She remained conscious until within a few minutes of the end, calmly discussing the approaching dissolution with her husband and a few friends who were present and made a will disposing of her property," the news stated.

Angus was severely burned in his efforts to rescue his beloved wife, and was still confined at the hospital during the funeral. The house had caught fire. The fire department responded promptly, but the building and contents were partially destroyed. Their home was in ruins — never to be a "home" now that his helpmate was gone forever.

The community was shocked by the accident. The Acantha stated, "In the history of Choteau a sadder fate has never come to any individual. The Bruce home was to be wired for electric lights the following day, and before she started to fill the lamp, Mrs. Bruce was heard to say, "'This is the last time I'll fill this lamp.'"

She died nine days shy of 20 years after having seen the meteor. 🏔

Library Evolution

The Choteau/Teton Public Library, at its choice down-town business location across the street from the court-house, gives no hint to the political drama and old-fash-ioned arm-twisting that occurred to put that important community resource in such a fitting and convenient place.

The Choteau Women's Club opened the first library in March 1917. In May 1931, they moved to a new library (now Mountain Front Market).

It became more difficult to operate as the years rolled on and the Choteau City Council came to their aid in May 1965 by accepting the property and creating a Choteau Public Library Board.

Soon, the Teton County Commissioners had set up a modest tax support system for the county's three libraries and the city of Choteau paid for its library's utilities and building maintenance.

Meanwhile, in August 1963, the Villager Hardware store and Tree Top Restaurant opened at that aforemen-tioned choice location on Main Avenue. It was a big place, 5,000 square feet with an eatery on the mezzanine.

The owners, however, filed for bankruptcy in July 1965 and eventually ceded the empty building to the First National Bank of Great Falls.

So it was that in October 1969 that Choteau Library Board members Mrs. Burr Huffman, Mrs. James Arens-meyer and Robert Nauck went public with their desire to buy the Villager, which the bank listed at $25,000. Another $5,000 was needed for furnishings, but the key domino was that the federal government would provide a 50/50 match.

The Friends of the Library concluded the problem was they didn't have any men to solicit funds. "It's not that it is below women to solicit funds," one of them said, "It's just that women can't do a good job of it."

With that, the Choteau Jaycees stepped in and decided to handle the solicitation led by a library committee of Adrian Dargan, Bill McCauley, Wayne Gollehon, Herb Foster, Reg Wearley, Dan Mayson, Charles Durr and Dr. Bill Patton.

As the Jaycees began raising the funds, the community learned that the federal funds were in jeopardy because of wrangling between Congress and the Nixon Administration. Choteau Mayor Jim Dellwo, however, reassured the community that even if a proposed $98,000 in federal funding was reduced to the state, the State Library Board had placed Choteau "number one" on the priority list for the $15,000 match.

As a goodwill gesture, the bank lowered the Villager's price from $25,000 to $22,000 on Nov. 27. The only hitch was a Jan. 2, 1970, deadline.

Working with a new goal of $13,500, the Jaycees urged the community to chip in. The group sponsored an open house in the building on Dec. 28, part of what Wearley called the "final library blast-off date." Pledges amounted to a little over $6,000, and the Jaycees decided it was time for house calls on Sunday.

As of Jan. 1 they had raised $11,000. With the goal so near, they convinced the bank to extend the time limit to Jan. 15. The "fever barometer" in the window of Citizens State Bank kept tabs as it rose to $11,700.

The March 5, 1970, Acantha front page sports a photo

of Jaycees member Jim Sherman presenting a $13,854 check to Huffman to buy the Villager. The group with the community's help fulfilled the promise made four months prior. In May, the federal match was on the way.

29

Death in Public Office

August 6, 2014

Blanche Jacobson's stint as the first woman to serve as the Teton County Clerk of District Court was bookended by the deaths of her predecessor and successor while serving in office.

The community was shocked on hearing of the sudden death of Paul Jacobson, 44, on Aug. 5, 1919. The Acantha reported that he was found on the road between Farmington and Choteau pinned underneath his car. The steering wheel rested on his back and he was conscious, but he lost consciousness while being transported to the hospital and died of internal injuries two hours later.

The wheel tracks indicated that he partially missed one bridge and overturned directly upon another nearby, thus blocking the road, the Acantha reported.

Paul Jacobson had served four years as deputy clerk of court under the late James Gibson, and upon Gibson's retirement in 1916, he became the Republican nominee for that office and was elected by a substantial majority. His term began Jan. 1, 1917.

On the day of Paul's death, the Teton County Commissioners appointed Paul's widow, Blanche, 35, to the office of Clerk of District Court, the first woman to serve in that office.

Blanche served until Dec. 31, 1932, running unopposed until the November 1932 election. She was the Republican nominee while Frances Carlson Rosengren was the

Democratic nominee.

"Surprises, upsets, tumbles, neck and neck races, thrills and sundry other things, all more or less bordering on the exciting order, characterized the great election Tuesday. On the main, the 'ins' fared badly regardless of party. Such, in short, is the story of the most engaging election Teton County has experienced in a number of years," the Acantha said.

The Democratic County Central Committee's election slogan that year was, "A Live Donkey is Better Than a Dead Elephant."

Blanche, 47, was an "in" and lost, 1,093 votes to 1,274 votes, in part because of the great national landslide that elected Democrat Franklin D. Roosevelt. Incumbent President Herbert Hoover carried both Choteau precincts by a small margin, but the county amassed 1,508 votes for Roosevelt and 876 for Hoover.

Before the election, Rosengren, a Teton County native and a college graduate, worked as a deputy in both the county treasurer's office and the county assessor's office. She was a widow with two teenage sons at the time of the election.

Rosengren began her first term on Jan. 1, 1933, but a year or so later, she became ill, and was diagnosed with cancer. She was absent from her office for about six weeks in the spring of 1936, and for a few weeks in the fall, but ran unopposed in the November election. She tried to carry on but her condition would not permit it, the Acantha reported.

The doctors at Deaconess Hospital in Great Falls found that the cancer was so far advanced and spread that it was impossible to do any good by operating. Rosengren returned to Choteau and died at age 39 on Jan. 2, 1937, at the home of her parents, John and Mary Carlson.

30

The Choteau Pavilion Steeped in History

November 1, 2006

The Choteau City Pavilion's blue-colored roof contrasted nicely in the fall of 2006 with the nearby City Park trees that sported a bright yellow color.

The park was quiet and so was the pavilion, but it was only in sleep mode, waiting for the next social event that might fill the space inside.

The pavilion has served as the center for social activities in this rural community for 85 years and counting. Starting with its debut on July 4, 1921, as the American Legion's "open-air pavilion," the unpretentious structure has served each generation in various ways. In turn, townsfolk, including the American Legion, roller-rink operators, the Lions Club, the Kiwanis, city officials and, most recently, the Pals of the Pavilion, have assessed the building and found ways and funds to adapt the structure to changing community needs.

The story of the pavilion begins when men of the two-year-old American Legion Choteau Post 6 met in Hodgskiss Hall to organize Memorial Day services in May 1921. A month later, the Choteau Acantha reported that construction of the open-air pavilion was nearly complete. At that time what would become the future City Park complex was divided into parcels with different owners: the Commercial Club park, the old fair grounds, private land and the Great

Northern Park.

Two months later, the biggest Fourth of July celebration that had ever been put on in the county took place, when an estimated 4,000 people participated in the day-long events that included dancing in the open-air pavilion in the afternoon and evening.

The Legion and the city gained a reputation that day for hosting a clean, fitting and pleasing program that went off without a hitch. "There never was a crowd better behaved," the Acantha reported. "There was little drunkenness and the fistic encounters which are so often a part of such a day, were conspicuous by their absence," penned the editor.

Thanks were given in part to the sheriff's deputies who had arrested three men the day before, entering the city limits in a Saxon roadster with three cases of whiskey concealed under the seats.

To be sure, Choteau's reputation was at stake. The American Legion pavilion wasn't the first "pavilion" in Choteau. Twenty-four years earlier, the Acantha, then published in Dupuyer, decried Choteau's pavilion as "the bad lands of Teton County where congregate all manner of bad men and women. It is a hotbed of debauchery and lewdness," the newspaper stated. Just when that building was torn down is not known, but the pavilion built in 1921 was off to a good start with the success of the July 4th celebration.

In August 1921, the Chautauqua, a respectable educational lecture series, was held in the pavilion.

The late Bob Zion, 86 in 2006, remembered attending the Chautauqua in the Legion's pavilion. Instead of glass windows, the pavilion had latched panels, hinged at the bottom. The panels opened out, held in place by chains.

The roof was simply rafters and roof board. During the Chautauqua, Zion's father, who was a skilled carpenter, removed the south center post after putting temporary jacks in the corners. That way, the stage was unobstructed, Zion said.

He recalled dances at the pavilion every Saturday night in those early years. "You could hear the music all over town," he said. More often than not, Zion, who played the saxophone and the clarinet, was one of the musicians.

The Elks Club in Great Falls would rent a special train that brought its members to the park for a picnic. Zion said the highlight for youngsters was the invitation to dive into a haystack that the Elks had salted with quarters, nickels and dimes.

"I met my wife roller skating there. She bumped into me and knocked me down," Zion said with a smile. He was about 19 at the time.

Choteau area senior George Higgins recalled more bits of pavilion history. His father, a World War I veteran, helped build the pavilion.

At some point, the Legion found it difficult to pay the property taxes on the building, and donated it to the city and at the same time started the rodeo on city grounds, signing a 100-year lease.

Higgins was in grade school when the skating started in the 1940s. He recalled that his sister was a good skater. The overhead heaters, since replaced, dated back to the 1940s when the Corbett brothers operated the roller skating rink in the pavilion.

"I remember, during World War II, they used old clamp-on skates," said Choteau senior Jack Reiding.

In September 1926, the first "Days of 49" jamboree found a home in the pavilion. In later years, the Choteau Lions Club resurrected the popular event at the pavilion to raise funds for the swimming pool.

Choteau resident Don LaBaugh remembered the "Days of 49'ers" in the early 1950s when the men in the town grew beards. He said, "I was 9 or 10. The Lions Club had a carnival with live geese. You were supposed to toss a ring to get it over the goose's head. I tried and tried, but I never could get the ring around their necks."

The pavilion cost $2,500 to build in 1921, and as the years went by, various groups made improvements. The late Choteau resident and past Lions Club Vice President Hank Smith, 81 in 2006, spearheaded the most significant change.

In 1948, Smith played saxophone in the community band. While playing for a two-night hospital benefit, he could hardly see the music sheets, he said. "I told myself that if I ever got to a point I could get a way to do something, I would, and that was in 1972," he recalled.

Although he was busy farming, Smith and Lions Club President Jack Rogers organized automobile raffles, and various other fundraisers to remodel the pavilion. They insulated and rewired the pavilion, put in windows, and fixed up the bathrooms that had been put in by the Square Dance Club after WWII.

Smith with his helpers, Rogers, Harry Luinstra and B.C. Colbenson, spent 1,000 hours remodeling the pavilion. "We had good help and got the electrical supplies and lumber at cost," Smith said.

Without the help, "I wouldn't have made it," he said. Smith built lower cabinets in the kitchen. Arvid Sundet, a carpenter who ran the local bowling alley, built the upper cabinets. The heaters were too high to heat the place and in the remodeling, Choteau senior Cal Southard lowered them. The Jaycees helped cut the false ceiling tiles that reduced on the noise.

"It's a nice place to have for the community, the Lions Club made it better," Higgins said.

When the pavilion needed a new roof in the early 1980s,

the Kiwanis stepped in. "I went to Kiwanis President Denny Perry and said 'Let's not hire anyone. We can do it with volunteers. We put on the north exposure in one day," said Harold Yeager of Choteau referring to the blue-colored metal roof.

People who weren't able to work on the roof bought the refreshments for the workers, Yeager said, adding, "When the community gets together and does it themselves the dollars go further."

For example, the maple floor is original, and the late Choteau senior citizen Ray Ginther and others spent hours refinishing it several years ago.

The Pals of the Pavilion, a grassroots group of county and city residents, say that it's time for the community to come together again to support needed improvements to the entrances, the kitchen and the bathrooms, among other things. An architectural assessment this summer detailed changes that would be necessary to bring the building into compliance with the Americans with Disabilities Act.

Pals Chairwoman Mar Sue Jensen said the group was seeking funds for remodeling. Besides working on the bathrooms and the kitchen, the Pals wanted to change the main entrance to the south end where a looped drive would allow people to drop off food and passengers. The Pals would work on eliminating the noisy heaters eventually, but first they wanted to move the bathrooms north and enlarge the kitchen.

A serving window in the kitchen would replace the long counter on the main floor.

"We want to preserve that building. It is used a lot," Jensen said in 2006.

The late Florence Weist, who moved to Choteau in the early 1940s, could attest to that. The Young Timers of Teton County met in the pavilion for dinner and dancing. "We had a lot of fun," she said in 2006, recalling that the Young Timers' annual get-together was the highlight of the year.

"We used to have prizes for dances and waltzes. We learned the two-step there," she said. A local group, the Rhythmaires, supplied live music and it was good music, she added.

"We have to keep things up or they deteriorate to a point they can't fix it," Weist said. "I love the setting of the pavilion. Let's not lose our one and only place where families can meet with its good, clean atmosphere," she added.

Weist looked forward to the day the Pals eliminated the suspended heating units and added a quieter furnace room.

"For as much as it's used, it is kept in pretty good shape. Choteau is very fortunate to have the pavilion," Weist said.

"It will be nice to see it remodeled. It's a wonderful thing for the community," Zion said.

"I think the city should keep it maintained. It benefits everybody," Smith said.

— 31 —

James Pulliam and the
J.C. Penney Co. Store

August 24, 31, September 7, 2016

Leaving behind a grueling job as a traveling shoe sales-man, Kentucky native James C. Pulliam, 39, got his big ca-reer break when he became the resident store manager at a new dry goods and clothing store in Choteau in April 1925.

Located in the McDonald block (where the antique store is now), the F.S. Jones Co. Golden Rule Chain Store was one of many stores in six states, the nearest ones being in Cut Bank, Havre and Big Sandy.

The Acantha reported his arrival on March 19, along with his wife, Fay, and daughter, Katherine, 13.

"In commenting upon Choteau and this section Mon-day Mr. Pulliam said that during the days when he traveled this territory he had often noted the beauty of Choteau and this valley and had more than once expressed a desire to live here, without thinking at the time that he ever would. He is confident that the Jones Co. store venture here will be a success and told local people that he is glad to be able to make his home in one of the best little towns in Montana," the Acantha said.

The Pulliams settled into the old Daley house in the Cowgill addition. Katherine made friends in school and James was invited on an elk hunt in November. The Acan-tha mentioned that Fay Pulliam had a medical issue the fol-lowing May 1926, but she was the heroine of the day when in July she was driving home with her daughter and some friends from a dance in Bynum and the rear axle broke at the foot of the hill near the C.O. Younce ranch, letting the back end of the car down onto the road. She maintained control of the vehicle and all escaped injury, the Acantha said.

The family vacationed in the Flathead Valley and in Glacier National Park and James Pulliam found time to be a cast member in a minstrel show in November 1926. He enjoyed going on buying trips to St. Paul and St. Louis, securing new merchandise for the store that advertised a different item each week in a good-sized display ad.

In May 1927 the Acantha announced, "Word has been received from J.C. Pulliam, manager of the F.S. Jones Co. Golden Rule store here, who is now in Minneapolis, that the J.C. Penney Co. has purchased the 54 stores owned by the Jones company and operating in Minnesota, Montana, North and South Dakota, Iowa and Wisconsin. Mr. Pulliam will be retained by the Penney organization as manager of the Choteau store."

The conversion of the local Jones store into a Penney Co. store was set to occur about June 1, 1927, but a large ad on June 9 stated that the complete change would not occur until about Aug. 1.

"Due notice will be given of the opening day under the new ownership. At that time the store will be completely stocked with new fresh crisp fall goods and the unexcelled buying resources of the J.C. Penney Co. will be yours to enjoy," the ad said.

While James Pulliam was busy with the store conversion, Fay Pulliam made a trip to Savannah, Missouri, to undergo treatment for cancer at the Dr. Nichols sanitarium.

The first large ad for the new Penney's store was on Aug. 4. "We're here and we want to get acquainted. It's rather lonesome when you first move to town, isn't it, so we want to get acquainted with our neighbors as soon as possible. Of course you know our manager and sales people, but you are probably wondering what sort of a store we plan to keep.

"Twenty-five years ago we started our business on the principle that everyone passing through our door should have a square deal and 100 cents worth for every dollar. Today there are 885 Penney stores scattered throughout 46 states, but our principles have never changed.

"We know that you will keep watch of our advertisements and window displays for each day will bring something of interest. As we never hold so called 'sales,' you are assured the same, fair consistently low prices every day in the year."

As the vacation period started, Mrs. O.G. Meadows joined the staff of clerks, and the Pulliam family was able to spend a week camping in the Sun River Canyon, but that break was not enough to prevent what happened next.

On Aug. 4, 1927, the Acantha published a large ad for the new Penney's store, with sales for workmen's "sox" for 15 cents and men's Oxfords for $3.98, among a long list of items.

Meadows was hired to fill in during the vacation period starting the first week of August, and the Pulliams set out for a two-week vacation in the Sun River Canyon and in Glacier National Park.

The Acantha noted that James's assistant, M.G. Carver, planned to leave with his family on James's return, for two weeks in the mountains near Townsend where his brother DeLoss had a cabin.

The summer's routine was broken when on Aug. 18 the Acantha reported that J.C. Pulliam, 41, was found dead from a gunshot wound on Aug. 17.

"Choteau was shocked yesterday morning by news of

the death of J.C. Pulliam, J.C. Penney's Co. store manager, who was found dead on the floor of the garage at the rear of his home with a bullet wound in his head and 22-caliber rifle lying on the floor by his side.

"The tragedy was discovered by Mrs. Pulliam shortly after 8 a.m. when, worried at her husband's absence from the house and her failure to reach him by telephone at the store, she went to the garage intending to take out their car and come downtown in search of him.

"Nothing in the nature of a message was found that would indicate any reason for Mr. Pulliam's act, but an investigation conducted by Coroner C.H. Connor, County Attorney Geo. Coffey Jr. and Dr. H.W. Bateman pointed clearly to suicide, Mr. Connor said, and resulted in the conclusion that an inquest was unnecessary. It is thought that Mr. Pulliam fired the fatal shot during a period of temporary derangement, brought on by worry," the Acantha stated.

The article continued with a report that Pulliam had "recently been working particularly hard on details incidental to the transfer of ownership of the store ... and the long hours and strain had worried him considerably, it was noticed by his family and friends."

More followed. Carver, "who had attended to much of the book work in connection with the newly installed Penney Co. system, left on his vacation, and Tuesday evening, Mrs. Pulliam told friends, Mr. Pulliam spoke of difficulty he had been having with his reports, saying that he felt as though, if the strain kept up, it would drive him crazy.

"Mrs. Pulliam urged him not to worry, but to get help on this work as he had Monday evening when he had called in W.G. Bloomdahl. Although he had worked late at the store Tuesday evening, he appeared in good spirits, it was said. He rose at the usual time yesterday morning, Mrs. Pulliam said, to kindle the kitchen fire, but remarked on rising that he had slept but little. She did not become alarmed, however, until she woke again about 8 a.m. and found that her husband had not dressed in his business clothes and was not in the house or at the store.

"Coupled with business worries was worry over the condition of the health of Mrs. Pulliam, who has not been well for several months and who only recently returned from a Missouri hospital where she had been undergoing treatment," the Acantha stated.

The article noted that none of his friends suspected from his behavior that he had reached the breaking point, and news of his tragic death was greeted with amazement and sorrow. Carver returned to temporarily run the store and James Pulliam was buried in Choteau Cemetery.

"County and city offices and business houses of the city were closed through the funeral hour as a mark of respect to the memory of the man who, during his two years and a half of residence here, had won the liking and esteem of his fellow citizens," the Acantha reported.

A week later, the Acantha stated that Connor had held an inquest after all, and the jury's verdict was that Pulliam came to his death by the accidental discharge of a gun.

A large J.C. Penney's display advertisement for merchandise appeared in the same issue of the Aug. 25, 1927, Acantha that reported on Pulliam's large funeral. The newspaper also reported that Mrs. Pulliam and her teenage daughter, Katherine, left for Spokane after the funeral to visit James's brother and family for a few weeks.

"They had not made any definite plans for the future," they told the Acantha. Their card of thanks was published on Sept. 1.

Then it was back to business, and on Sept. 15, the Acantha reported that the Penney store planned to enlarge its space, according to the new manager W.B. Condran from

Huron, South Dakota. The store was located in the McDonald block where the antique store is now, but it had not yet expanded north into the corner space where a drug store was then located. The 1927 remodeling, however, expanded the space to the south and provided an entrance on the north side in addition to the one on the east side.

Fay Pulliam and her daughter returned to Choteau with an announcement that they would spend the winter in Washington state, and in the meantime, they would rent an apartment in the Larson building. The Acantha published the Pulliam estate's probate notice along with a classified ad, "For sale Buick touring car in good condition. Reasonable, Mrs. F.T. Pulliam, Room 16 Larson blk."

Coroner Connor's end of year report noted that he had collected five coins from James's body when he was found dead in his garage, and the money was returned to his wife.

The next reference on the Pulliams appeared the following July 1928, reporting that the two women were living in Great Falls and Katherine had come up for a visit with friends in Choteau, the houseguest of Mrs. Frank Curtis.

The community knew that Fay Pulliam had been ill at the time of her husband's death, so it was a surprise on Nov. 29, 1928, when the Acantha reported that Fay had wed a divorced pastor.

Mrs. Pulliam and the Rev. Dr. H. Styles Harris, "recent pastor of the First Methodist Church in Great Falls, were married at Ritzville, Washington, Nov. 10, which was one day after the minister's first wife divorced him here in Choteau. It is reported that they will reside in California, though the minister prior to leaving Great Falls announced that he would enter the University of Mexico to take a course in psychiatry, the science of mental derangements," the Acantha said.

A year, almost to the day after that, the Acantha

reported that Fay Pulliam Harris, 39, had died in San Diego, California. The newspaper repeated the widow's timing of her second marriage, and ended with this comment, "The episode led to Mr. Harris quitting the ministry and the revocation of ordination papers. He announced at the time that he would enter the University of Mexico to pursue a course in psychiatry, but whether he ever did has not been learned here."

Katherine, 17, now an orphan, is listed in the 1930 census as a "lodger" in San Diego. Nothing more could be gleaned from the old newspapers.

The Penney's store prospered, however, but with a series of managers. Most of them moved on when promoted to a bigger store somewhere else.

By June 1935 the Penney's store had celebrated the eighth anniversary of its founding in Choteau. Manager Ken Sturgis resigned in October 1938 to go into business for himself and eventually served three terms as Choteau mayor.

Penney's expanded north into the corner of the McDonald building in February 1945 when the Rexall Drug Store and Malone Pharmacy moved to the Larson building.

More remodeling under different managers took place after that, and in March 1947 2,000 people attended an open house. Manager and WWII veteran Jim Henderson was in the post until June 1957.

Gale Isakson was the Penney store manager for six years, but then he moved to Utah in August 1967 to manage a store there. Mic Darnold was manager for only a year when the Penney's store that had served the city and county for 41 years, announced it would close Dec. 31, 1968.

Penney District Manager Paul Brunner said it was to be regretted, but "with the corporation tax and the cost of doing business today, the company could not justify the capital expenditure necessary to bring the store up to company standards."

Isakson came back to Choteau and opened a department store in March 1969 with 1,000 people attending the open house. But that's another story.

— 32 —

Cemetery Grounds

February 4, 2015

In 2015 came the news that the Teton County Commissioners had hired a contractor to remove about 70 trees in the Choteau Cemetery that were dead or dying. It prompted a look back at the time when they were planted.

The big push to beautify the then 44-year-old cemetery came in early 1927 when the Choteau City Council agreed to furnish a water supply to the cemetery, sufficient for irrigating purposes, and to build a proposed four-inch line that would insure ample water for the trees set out to border the cemetery enclosure.

In April 1927, the council arranged for a levy that would help pay the $4,600 cost to run 4,000 feet of new main, and the cemetery board raised the price of lots to help finance improvements.

The board also published a notice to all lot owners to "meet at the cemetery at 9 a.m. on May 26 bringing shovels, rakes and a team or two if possible, for the purpose of removing surplus dirt and cleaning up the cemetery grounds in preparation for Memorial Day."

Pacific States Cast Iron Pipe Co. of Provo, Utah, had the low bid for the pipe and Harold M. Burrell and H.O. Vandewark had the winning bid to do the excavation work.

That done, the following spring, City Clerk John Moore purchased 300 pounds of lawn grass seed, rose bushes of the "Prairie King" variety and one dozen Black Hills spruce from Treadwell Nursery in Great Falls. Together with hundreds of green ash trees from Choteau's own nursery at the north end of town, the plan just awaited good weather.

"Surprises are in store for many others if they will visit the graveyard — but presently it will be more than a 'grave' yard," the Acantha reported on April 26, 1928. "It will be a yard of trees and green grass and flowers and a design rather than a hodge podge. ...

"A good start was made on the work last week, and this week it went forward by leaps and bounds. On Monday 150 trees had been planted, and before the job is finished between 400 and 500 will be planted. An even dozen Black Hills spruce have been set out and four-dozen rose bushes will be added.

"A new entrance has been made to the cemetery, placing it in the center of the north and south line on the west, [sic, east] which makes it about 100 feet farther south than the old one. A public drinking fountain will be erected near the entrance. Leading from the entrance the road divides right and left in graceful curves. In the plot this created by the two roads, and immediately in front of the entrance, will be a fountain surrounded by rose bushes and the evergreen trees.

"A corner of the cemetery on the southeast will be used for deceased soldiers only, one grave already being situated in that section. The entire south side of the cemetery has been plowed and leveled. It is being platted, and trees will be set out and lawn grass sown. A good portion of the east side has also been plowed and will be similarly treated.

"Improvement work is also contemplated on the older portions of the burying ground, but this cannot be done with the regularity of design, which will characterize the work in the newer parts. Because many lots in the cemetery are now owned by individuals, it is impossible for the city to go ahead with the same freedom exercised in other portions."

The May 31, 1928, Acantha beamed that for Memorial Day, "the cemetery presented a beautiful appearance with its new embellishments and ornamentation."

Surely it became a beautiful resting place for the likes of John Billings, said to be the first burial. A letter from Choteau businessman A.B. Hamilton published in the April 7, 1883, Benton Weekly Record read, "I write to tell you that John Billings died at my house at one o'clock today. He had been quite sick for three weeks. Poor fellow, he is out of trouble now. He was 55 years and two months old. Served three years during the war when he contracted lung disease. Was a member of the Territorial Legislature while the Capital was at Virginia City, and was assessor for a portion of Lewis & Clark County several years ago. He has been living with me about 10 years."

— 33 —
1930s

June 26, 2013

After scanning through the Acantha newspapers from the 1930s, Jeanne Anderson noticed that no matter how much time has passed, some things have remained the same after 80 years, but then again it's not too often that one is invited to a hanging.

"Starting in the 1930s the Lions Club was so active what with raising funds for the swimming pool. I noticed how active it was then and still is. That impressed me," said, Anderson, who volunteered to gather the news highlights from the 1930s for the Choteau Centennial in 2013.

She said the American Legion was also very active in doing things for the community because it owned what is now the Choteau Pavilion in the City Park and hosted many events and fundraisers to maintain it. Also active in the 1930s was the Choteau Woman's Club that operated a community library.

Anderson recalled reading that the Choteau Country Club listed who played and what were the scores in the Acantha, the club having purchased the grounds in 1933 from the James Sulgrove estate. A variety of stores and shops in the 1930s occupied every nook and cranny on Main Avenue and a block east and west, even though the Great Depression had begun.

"The prices were low, that goes without saying," she said. Among the firsts for Choteau were the airport being established in 1934, then abolished; and the Lions Club swimming pool being built. The first July 4th fireworks began in 1935.

The wife of the late Don Anderson, and a longtime history buff, Jeanne hails from Dupuyer where her daughter Susan Anderson with Stan Brown Jr. operate the family ranch. Jeanne said it took a considerable amount of time weeding through the Acanthas to get the news highlights because she spent much time reading the material that mentioned Dupuyer. All in all, it was a good project, she said.

Perhaps the most notorious event of the decade was the execution by hanging of George Hoffman on July 28, 1933, the gallows having been transported from Butte. He was convicted in the 1932 murder of George Burrell, proprietor of the Club. His appeal of the conviction to the Montana Supreme Court was unsuccessful. The sheriff sent out invitations to the hanging at the county jail.

The city hall was built in 1933, the building having been paid for with funds from the water department, making it a fact that the water users, not taxpayers paid for it.

— 34 —

Chinese Immigrant Soo Son

January 3, 2018

By the time Chinese immigrant Soo Son was the honored guest at a banquet at the Beaupre Hotel in August 1933, he had spent 44 years in Teton County, first employed as a cook for Sands and Taylor on the S.T. ranch, and later as a restaurant owner in Choteau.

He bought the Gem Restaurant in December 1902 from Mrs. Ed. Dennis and updated her ad to say, "The Gem Restaurant. Soo Son, prop. First class restaurant. Meals at all hours. Bread for sale." He tried to sell it in 1904, but with no buyers, he continued to run it, although he got embroiled in the Acantha's partisan condemnation of Sheriff George C. Taylor's run for reelection alleging favoritism in taking juries exclusively to Soo Son's restaurant.

After a vacation to San Francisco in the spring of 1907, he returned with his new wife, "a handsome Chinese woman." The couple ran the Gem Restaurant for another year, but left for Helena in July 1908. They are listed in the 1910 Helena census, where Soo Son, 46, and wife, Soo Son She, 20, operate a Chinese general store.

They came back to Choteau in August 1913, bought a house and thereafter Soo owned a restaurant off and on until about 1930. The January 1920 federal census lists Soo Son, 59, a cook in a restaurant, with his wife, Rosie, 29, born in California. (The census data is not consistent as to their ages.)

His wife was never mentioned after that. In July 1928

Soo was reported to be cooking for the Beaupre Hotel Café, but in February 1930 he had a slight stroke of paralysis, which affected his left side. He sold his restaurant to George Benedict and retired. He turned 70 on Oct. 4.

The banquet in Soo's honor in August 1933 was to bid him farewell.

"When a former Montana governor (now U.S. senator), a state senator, a mayor, a group of business and professional men and other friends both old and young, sit down to a banquet table to honor an old [man from China] and bid him farewell as he returns to his mother land with the avowed intentions of never returning and presumably to die, then there's something more than even the unordinary," the Acantha reported.

The former governor present was Sen. John E. Erickson, the state senator, Tom Larson, and the mayor, C.W. Burns. Larson was toastmaster, Erickson was the principal speaker, and (Soo Son) himself, was one of those who gave thanks, the paper said.

"From the lips of all came praise — praise for his citizenship — though he could never claim that privilege; praise for his charity; praise for his honesty; praise for his fairness with all people; praise for his law abiding qualities; praise for humor and fellowship; praise for his love of children. What person could live in a community for 44 years and leave it without an enemy, the former governor declared, as he recalled his early acquaintanceship with Soo Son in the days when he (the speaker) was a young attorney here. 'All they said to me when I left was "goodbye" and many were glad to get rid of me at that,' Sen. Erickson said.

"But there was more than speechmaking. He was presented with a new hat, a new sweater, a box of cigars, a purse to buy himself something with when he reaches San Francisco, and yesterday morning, Arthur Hirshberg sent him to Great Falls by auto and was an attendant to see him safely on the train.

"That ended Soo Son's career in Choteau," the paper reported. Soo Son told the paper he didn't plan to come back because he was getting too old.

The community waited until July 1958 to hear news of Soo from Arthur Wong, a nephew of Soo's wife, who was a Choteau visitor. "Soo Son, he said, lived for about two years after he left Choteau. He saved his earnings in order to live in grand style at his former home in Canton, China. When he returned there, he married a 19-year-old girl, whose parents were glad to betroth their daughter to a well-to-do American.

"The climate did not agree with Soo Son, who was in his 70s and died about a year after his return to Canton. After his death, said Wong, the bride became entangled in a legal suit over Soo Son's estate, which was being contested by an elderly son of Soo Son by a previous marriage."

35

The Darkest Days

June 12, 2013

The darkest days of World War II were also some of the coldest days on record, according to Choteau Centennial volunteer Ruth Reiquam who gathered news highlights from the 1940s.

"Lots of deaths of prominent people and lot of casualties in the war. It was a subdued July 4th, no rodeo; the whole country was subdued," Reiquam recalled.

Reiquam and a handful of other volunteers assisted Centennial Committee member Nancy Thornton in preparing a list of the most significant news of each decade since 1913 when Choteau incorporated as a town. It became a city a few years later when the population numbered more that 1,000 residents.

"There was only so much sugar allowed, and you had a sticker for your car for gasoline. Meat, butter and shoes were also rationed. I remember that, because shoes were one thing I liked," Reiquam said, recalling her early years living in Choteau and Dutton.

She remembered getting a scuffed toe from riding her bike and how her mother became upset, scolding her for not being careful.

Reiquam said it was a bit tedious going through the Choteau Acantha newspapers looking for highlights from the 1940s, but rather than getting on with the task, she was often "waylaid reading other stuff." Still, she said she enjoyed learning about the era.

The year 1943, for example, began with Civilian Defense Chairman John Dale ordering a practice blackout on Jan. 13 at 7 p.m. Then a cold snap lowered the temperature to 44 degrees below zero on Jan. 24, but not before 14 inches of snow had fallen.

Barney McClue, who had been reported missing in 1942, was reported alive as a Japanese prisoner of war, and Navy man Terry Tennant, stationed in England, was reported killed, only to be listed as a survivor a week later.

A.B. Guthrie Jr. turned author with his new book, "Murders at Moon Dance."

In April 1943 longtime dentist E.J. Crary had a fatal cerebral hemorrhage. The shocked townsfolk turned out in huge numbers to attend his funeral.

Instead of a celebration, Choteau held an "open house" on July 4, 1943. Because of the war conditions, no large celebration was planned. The activities included use of the City Park, swimming pool, tennis courts and golf links. Free coffee was served in the park.

Then in August, an early morning shooting endangered the lives of many people. The Acantha reported that a man "shot up" the Parkway Café, fired at an officer and threatened the life of Gladys Riggs. Sheriff Al Peterson then shot him.

Choteau's centennial history is online. Search for it to learn more.

36

War Casualties

November 11, 2015

Nov. 11 is a day to honor American veterans. During years of conflict the Acantha brought the news of those who were casualties as learned from letters and telegrams that made every citizen grieve. Here are a few of those men who died in World War II far from home.

Second Lt. Charles "Bud" Hallberg was killed in France on Aug. 7, 1944. A former assistant cashier at the Citizens State Bank, and a Choteau ex-basketball star, Hallberg became a combat pilot in a "speedy pursuit plane," the Acantha said. By May 1944 he was in England and in his letter published at that time he appeared upbeat for having not gotten seasick on the way over. By Nov. 7, a telegram informed his parents he was dead.

Choteau High School graduate Donald E. Jacobson, 19, died on Okinawa on June 16, 1945. On the day he was killed, his critically ill father died in a Great Falls hospital.

State Sen. Paul Rice of Pendroy learned that his son, Sgt. George E. Rice, was killed in Africa in March 1943. Members of the state Senate rose and stood in silence with bowed heads for a few moments, after which there was a short memorial service as a token of respect, the Acantha said.

Power High School graduate and Marine Donald Paulus, 19, was killed on Saipan in the South Pacific and Acantha readers learned of his death on July 20, 1944.

Army pilot Norman A. Rosengren of Pendroy died on

July 28, 1945, in India. "Rosie was an outstanding athlete and member of the basketball, track and football team," the Acantha noted. He had gradated in 1940 or 41 and had a wife and son.

Sgt. Henry B. Haralson 24, drowned in the China Sea. A graduate of Dutton High School, Henry had enlisted in March 1940 in the Coast Guard artillery. He was assigned to the Philippines and taken prisoner at the fall of Bataan early in 1942.

Everett C. Leech from Bynum was taken prisoner at Corregidor and it was a long time before his people heard anything from him, the Acantha said. Then came a card released from a Japanese prison camp.

Haralson and Leech were on the same ship, the Arisan Maru, on Oct. 24, 1944, carrying at least 1,778 American prisoners of war including 26 men from Montana.

According to the late William Bowen who did extensive research on the event and that is published on the internet, "Naval records indicate that the USS Shark II (SS 314) attacked a Japanese freighter in the late afternoon of Oct. 24, 1944. The USS Shark was lost with all 87 hands in that same action and is believed to have torpedoed the Arisan. The Arisan carried no markings or flag indicating that it was carrying Allied prisoners. The Americans had no way of recognizing the Arisan as a prison ship."

Bowen goes on to say, "Regardless of the final count, the Arisan still represents the greatest loss of American life in a single military sinking. Approximately 5,000 American men died on 'hell ships' in transit from the Philippines to Japan. The total is over 20,000 men lost when considering all Allied prisoners on Japanese hell ships traveling in the Pacific. If they were not killed by friendly fire in the fog of war by Allied planes and submarines, they died in the filthy holds of the freighters carrying them to Japan for forced labor."

Pfc. Milton H. Talifson grew up in Bynum and Farmington and took his physical exam in Butte on Dec. 14, 1942, to enter the Army. He died in December 1944 at age 28 in Germany.

His buddies sent his mother a letter that the Acantha published in March 1945. They said Milton was killed right after Christmas during an air raid. A bomb exploded near and shrapnel killed him instantly and painlessly. It happened very quickly and he was unaware of any danger, they said.

The letter said in part, "None of us know how to write this letter, and in writing it we may be bringing you more grief, ... but you can feel awfully proud of Milton. None of us can say anything but to his credit. We have borrowed his clothes, shared our cigarettes, our packages, our good times; we have worked together under all kinds of conditions, and he had proved himself entirely unselfish and capable of doing more than his share. None of us would have felt the loss more, if he had been a brother."

— 37 —

Bud Olson on D-Day

September 19, 2007

Staff Sgt. Bud Olson looked up from his map of Normandy through the glider window to the beach below and drew strength from everything he had learned since he had volunteered for overseas duty in November 1943.

The date was D-Day-plus one, June 7, 1944, and Olson was 500 feet in the air above Utah Beach, the codename for the westernmost of five landing beaches on the shores of France. It was a long way from where Olson had grown up on a ranch 15 miles south of Great Falls.

Olson was inducted in the Army in August 1942. After a variety of duties in the 80th Division, he volunteered for overseas duty in the 101st Airborne Division. In the fall of 1943 in London, his battalion commander was impressed with Bud's smarts (he could type, knew shorthand and had studied military law) and he sent Olson to classes on German small arms, aircraft identification, and glider tactics, among other things. About this time, the 101st Airborne Division reorganized and created three glider battalions. Olson's new unit was 5th company of the 3rd Battalion, 325 Glider Infantry of the 82nd Airborne Division.

In February 1944, Olson was posted in the Supreme Headquarters of the Allied Expeditionary Force in London where he studied maps of the Normandy peninsula for six weeks. He was the only enlisted man in his battalion, with five officers, who knew about the coming invasion — where, but not when. Back at his base, Olson led many briefings on what he had learned while in London.

"It kept me busy. I was restricted to camp during this period due to my classification. I have always considered this an honor," Olson said in a letter recalling his service.

After training on gliders without a break, Olson's unit moved to Exeter, England, one of the D-Day staging areas, during the last part of May 1944. Olson was ready to ride in the lead glider of his battalion, with 55 gliders following. He was well trained in map reading, having daily studied the aerial photos taken by the reconnaissance pilots looking for German troop movements and new fortifications.

German soldiers had occupied France for four years, plenty of time to pepper the land with antiaircraft guns.

Flying above the English Channel on the way to Normandy, Olson and 27 other soldiers sat uneasily on board the British-built "Horsa" No. H-14, a glider made mostly of plywood, being towed by a C-47 airplane.

His map reading skills put Olson in the nose of the glider ready to direct the pilot to the landing zone. His pocket contained an "escape kit," given to only certain soldiers, and given on the promise that if he were captured, Olson would kill himself. The contents included some French money, a silk map of France, a Bullova watch, a French dictionary and a cyanide pill.

Looking down, Olson had time to recognize Utah Beach, before he was jerked out of his study of the invasion below. Ahead, the tow plane burst into flames, having been hit by flack. As Olson looked on, the glider pilot cut loose the towline and the glider was free, descending into God-knows-where, too soon to land in the designated LZ.

Floating down, Olson was aware of the silence except for the sound of the wind, then nothing. He awoke with a glider wheel resting on his chest; his legs cut and bleeding. His glider had crash-landed a few miles northeast of

Sainte-Mere-Eglise, the first town to be liberated. Olson had fallen through the plane to the ground as the glider careened across a field into a forest, breaking apart. Olson was the only survivor.

As Olson hobbled to an aid station to get patched up, he was reminded of the speech Gen. Eisenhower gave to the men on the eve of the invasion. The general told them there would be 30 percent casualties on landing. "Sell your life dearly," the general said. Olson held back his response. He wanted to tell Eisenhower he didn't want to sell his life.

The battalion had landed in amongst a group of German soldiers, who chose their own destiny. Some wanted to fight and some wanted to surrender, but Olson saw that the Americans had a lot of firepower handy.

Olson spent the rest of the day in a defensive position with other soldiers waiting for the sun to set, wondering whether the news reports of the largest airborne assault in history had reached his sweetheart, Vi, back in Great Falls.

Walking through Sainte-Mere-Eglise at one point, Olson saw a paratrooper hanging on the church steeple. From what Olson could see, the man was dead, but the legend lives on that the man was only feigning death.

Walking toward Chef duPont the next day, Olson could hear the American naval shells flying overhead and landing nearby. His company had been instructed many times never to lunch in large groups, but Olson and his buddies decided they were safe where they sat behind a hill in the ditch below the road grade.

They stopped chewing to listen, and heard the sound of a shell coming in very low. It tore through the road fill and landed near the group, but it was a dud and didn't explode. "Lucky for us. We learned our lesson," Olson said, writing later about the incident.

On June 9, Olson saw his first action. Ordered to cross a

causeway on the Merderet River three miles west of Sainte-Mere-Eglise, at La Fiere, the 5th company immediately ran into intense enemy fire.

With General Ridgway urging them on, one soldier after another fell, trying to force the 400-yard crossing. Olson started running and pretty soon no one was in front, and he went into the ditch, but soon he and other soldiers eliminated a dug-in German machine gun that had caused so many causalities.

Major Moore took over after the battalion commander was relieved. After Moore was wounded in the neck, Olson dressed the wound for his commander. Moore refused to be evacuated and kept going. The bridgehead was established.

During the afternoon, the company had a serious counter attack. Seeing a German mortar lying near his men, Moore told Olson, "I sent you to a school on German arms, use this mortar to prove it. Olson said later he probably never hit anything when he fired the shell, but he did what he was told.

When night fell, Olson re-crossed the causeway, evading sniper fire, located a unit that was to relieve his company and led them across.

"I have always said that I was one of the few GIs who had to cross the Merderet River three times in one day," Olson wrote later.

Moore was evacuated and Major Gardner took command. On June 13, the company was attacking near St. Sauveur Le Vicomte, about 10 miles west of Sainte-Mere-Eglise. The command post was located in a deep ditch and from there, four men were watching the attack, Major Gardner, Capt. Metlick, radio operator King and Olson.

As Olson moved a short ways away for a reason he would never remember, a German mortar shell landed among the three others, killing them. After the battle, the three casualties were not accounted for and Olson, the only survivor, led the grave registration officer back to the site.

On June 14, Major Leahy took over the command of the battalion and he held that position until the war was over.

Another battle, another causeway, crossing the La Douve River, the battalion found itself in a defensive position near Pretot and set up a command post in a stone building from June 16 to June 24.

Owing to the heavy casualties, Olson was appointed to fill the vacancy of battalion Sgt. Major. He became an aide to the battalion staff and kept a daily log on what went on. He also carried a camera, which was against regulations.

The command post came under mortar attack twice, the second time just after Olson snapped a photo of five fellow soldiers, three of whom were killed instantly. The unit determined that a local citizen was a collaborator providing the Germans with the command post locations. The man paid dearly for helping the enemy.

On the night of June 21, Major Leahy ordered Olson to lead a patrol to try to locate enemy replacements. The patrol encountered enemy fire and was pinned down for quite a while, before it could continue the patrol, finish the job and get back to headquarters safely. (Olson was awarded a Bronze star for that action.)

On July 12, Olson was relieved and returned to England, having spent 36 days in Normandy. He later participated in the invasion of Holland.

At the comfortable home that Olson, 86, shares with Vi on the Teton River northwest of Choteau, Bud has time to reminisce about the war that happened more than 60 years ago. He still has the silk map and Bullova watch he carried in Normandy, although the crystal is broken. He brought them out of storage on the eve of his return to France, a journey taken to describe what happened for the writers of a documentary that the National World War II Museum in New Orleans, Louisiana, is making about the Causeway Battle of La Fiere.

Olson is one of thousands of former American servicemen and women who will be watching Ken Burns' chronicle of the war on PBS this weekend.

———————

Retired Choteau area rancher and World War II veteran Bud Olson flew to Normandy, France, on Aug. 3, 2007, to participate in the filming of a documentary* about the Battle at the La Fiere Causeway.

"I was so glad I went. I'd been thinking about it for years," Olson, 86, said in an interview after he returned home on Aug. 12.

Olson traveled with his daughter, Judy Stewart of Billings, while Bud's wife, Vi, stayed home, near the computer and a telephone, which Bud used almost daily.

Bud and Judy stayed at a bed and breakfast in Sainte-Mere-Eglise, where Bud was the guest of the filmmaker. The director of the National WWII Museum in New Orleans invited Olson on the expenses-paid trip, along with five other veterans who participated in the June 9, 1944, battle at La Fiere, one of several battles to secure passage over the Merderet River.

The veterans spent each day being followed around by a PBS film crew and their evenings at various banquets and commemorations within a 20-square-mile area where the D-Day invasion began so long ago.

———————

* The documentary, "Seize & Secure: The Battle for La Fiere," made its broadcast premiere on June 6, 2019, on PBS, part of the National WWII Museum's commemoration of the 75th anniversary of D-Day. The DVD is available for sale at the Museum store's webpage.

Olson was the youngest man of the group. He reflected later that the opportunity to be in Normandy again was special. "Some day I would have run out of options," he said, explaining that he had not reached the point that he was too old or frail to go. "I'm so happy it all worked out," he said.

Sainte-Mere-Eglise was the first town liberated and it draws tourists from all over the world today. Olson and the other veterans wore the cap of their units, Bud's being the 82nd Airborne Division, and nearly everyone who saw him, asked him to pose for a picture, Judy doing the honors as the photographer, snapping one picture after another, a different camera each time.

Although there was some free time, the filming was exhausting. The veterans would assemble in the morning, learning where they were to go, and tell what happened at that spot in front of the camera. Olson said he was interviewed twice, the first interview lasting three and a half hours. "We always had a mike clipped to our shirts," Olson said.

Seeing the La Fiere causeway after 63 years, Olson was surprised by the changes. He remembered how the Germans has flooded the fields on both sides of the causeway over the Merderet River, turning the 400-yard-long road into a shooting gallery that took many American causalities. At one point, Olson was directed to lie down in the exact spot where he had sought cover in a ditch.

During the filming, Olson marked a personal milestone. "I always said I crossed the causeway three times in one day. Now add four more, for seven times," he said.

The causeway is still there, but it is a beautiful highway now, a ribbon linking grass-covered fields between beautiful farms and trees planted in rows. "The difference is black and white. I never saw such a manicured countryside. They must sweep the roads," Olson said.

Still, the memories of the invasion are preserved in nearly every house in Normandy. On several occasions people invited Bud and Judy into their homes, or around back of them to see their war exhibits, — pieces of guns, parachutes, shell casings, pictures of corpses, — the war is still very real for the folks there.

During one free morning, Bud and Judy met a French historian who once taught at the University of Montana. He is writing a book, and with maps in hand, they all set off to find the place where Bud's glider had crash-landed. The landowner met the group, then showed Bud his war display that included "asparagus sticks," long poles set at a angle used to impale gliders that landed.

In one village, Gen. Patton's granddaughter, living in one of the many castles still standing in Normandy, showed Bud and Judy her museum of war artifacts.

On another free morning, a Frenchman took the pair to Utah Beach. Standing there, Bud could not believe how pristine it is kept by the townsfolk, again, as if it were manicured. Looking down, though, Bud saw the telltale sign of the war, a bit of rusted barbed wire.

Bud and Judy also visited the cemetery at Omaha Beach, where many of fallen of the 82nd and 101st Army Airborne are buried. "We tried to find people in the register. I didn't sleep the night before thinking about names," Bud said. He later found two people from his battalion.

For hundreds of tourists, the hung-up paratrooper on the church steeple at Sainte-Mere-Eglise is the most important photo to obtain on their trip to Normandy. "I saw that thing hanging two days after D-Day. Everyone's impression is different," Olson said, acknowledging the famous tale about the man, John Steele, who said he was the paratrooper feigning death.

At the rear of the bed and breakfast where Bud and Judy stayed in Sainte-Mere-Eglise, a circle of glass bricks marks the spot of an old well where a paratrooper drowned, having dropped into it on D-Day.

In the town's sidewalk cafes, the first thing asked of visiting veterans is to sign wooden paddles affixed to the walls. Everyone recognizes veterans and offers friendly greetings. "I have never been kissed so much in my life, kissed on both sides of my cheeks," Bud said, with a smile.

It took a while to adjust to the eight-hour time change, but they never got used to the late and long dining that the French love. They did try the goose liver, one dish of five courses during one of several banquets they attended. Bud brought home a bottle of Calvados, a strong French wine he plans to open on his 100th birthday.

In Paris, Bud and Judy stayed in a place six blocks from the Eiffel Tower, but the lines were too long to get a ticket. They went on a bus tour instead and took lots of pictures, ending up at the Arc de Triomphe. Souvenirs in hand, the two world travelers looked at each other and said, "Let's go home," Bud recalled.

The Air France flight took them over London, Iceland, and Greenland as they headed for Detroit, Michigan, and along the way on a tiny screen, Bud could follow the jet's progress, the altitude and the outside temperature. That amazing bit of technology impressed Olson, who 63 years earlier had crossed that first leg in a plywood glider.

But the best thing of all, Bud concluded, was getting to the Great Falls Airport where he found Vi waiting, the same woman who had waited for him to return from the war those many years ago.

"I sure missed her," he said.

— 38 —

Dog Poisoners

June 13, 20, 27, and July 4, 11, 2018

Whenever it happened, the folks in Choteau felt an unease that someone living in their midst could do such a heartless and cruel thing, but over the years the dog poisoners got away with it.

The Choteau Calumet reported in February 1889, "A valuable hound, belonging to Louis Morgan was poisoned on Monday last by some unknown person whose health will require a change of climate if Louis ever spots him."

The next mention was in the Dupuyer Acantha in July 1897. "The dog poisoner has made the rounds of Dupuyer and has made quite a clean-up. Some day this individual will be found out, and he is liable then to get a dose of his own medicine."

The Teton Chronicle in Choteau in the fall of 1897 reported, "J.W. Armstrong had two bird dogs poisoned — one Friday night and the other Saturday night. He says he will give $50 cash for information leading to the conviction of the guilty party."

"Dog poisoning seems to be a fad in Choteau," the paper said in December 1897. "There does appear to be a large number of dogs in town, but then it must be remembered that some of them are quite valuable, being the property of sheepherders, who are spending the winter in town. The perpetrators will be severely dealt with if their identity is made known."

The paper continued, "The dog poisoner is abroad in

town, judging from the number of dead dogs laying around in the alleys and upon the commons. Something should be done to abate the nuisance, especially since the weather has turned warm."

The Acantha wrote on Jan. 27, 1898, "Bynum, not to be out done by Dupuyer and Choteau, has a dog poisoner, and as a result several valuable dogs are dead."

Over the years the culprits remained a mystery, and only one person was convicted of the deed back in the old days. In January 1898 Joseph Brown, manager of McKnight's store at Dupuyer, pled guilty to scattering poison in Dupuyer and Choteau with the intention of poisoning dogs. Dupuyer Township Justice of the Peace George Magee fined him $25 and costs. He left for the Klondike shortly after that.

In July 1899, it happened again. The Montanian reported, "Contempt for the 'yaller dog' is well-nigh universal, but this, like other general rules, has its exceptions. Jack Gordon, for instance, is, or rather was, a great admirer of his yellow dog, Prince, that succumbed to a dose of poison one day last week.

"Specifically he has not very much to say in the dead dog's favor though he does say that he never picked a quarrel with a friendly dog or turned tail to a hostile one. Mr. G. is very much down on the man that administered the poison to his favorite Prince. He does not swear about him because he does not swear about anything, but he does express the belief that this poisoner whoever he is will sometime go where the wicked never cease having trouble and the weary sinner never finds rest."

In February 1901, the Montanian reported, "Several dogs have been poisoned lately and some of them are valuable ones. The owners are determined that the miscreants who poisoned their valuable dogs shall be punished if possible. Dog poisoners should remember there is a law covering the subject and that the officials stand ready to enforce it."

After that and for more than 30 years, the Choteau newspapers made no mention of dog poisoners, but on Dec. 29, 1932, Acantha publisher E.L. Jourdonnais, let it rip. He did not mention that any dogs had died, but something must have prompted his post.

"The Dog Poisoner. ... The perversities of human beings are exemplified in numerous ways. We sometimes read of those who delight in torture and of others whose joy is in willful destruction of property in such a way as to cause misery or loss to another. But of all the despicable exemplifications of depravity in man, that of the willful dog poisoner is among the worst. A rattlesnake warns with his rattle before he strikes and a skunk hoists his colorful tail high above him, that he may be seen and let alone. But the dog poisoner skulks in the night or working in daylight, is so stealthy in his movements that to uncover evidence against him is usually an impossibility." His tirade continued for several more paragraphs.

"To analyze the traits of a dog poisoner is a problem for the psychologist," he said in the Dec. 29 editorial. "To him a dog is just another dog. To the person who owns the dog, that dog is an exemplification of loyalty, devotion, faithfulness, playfulness and companionship. The former sees nothing of these virtues and he cares less. Possibly the dog has caused him some temporary annoyance, but the chances are 100 to one that this is more fanciful than real and that the owner of the dog would gladly take corrective measures if apprised of the nuisance.

"Our law recognizes that there must be responsibility connected with the ownership of dogs, and therefore licenses and other regulations are provided.

"By the same token it recognizes that the legal and responsible owner of a dog is entitled to protection as instanced in the above quotation. There may be maudlin and perverted sentimentality regarding dogs, and where such is the case a mongrel dog or a pack of curs are likely to be a community nuisance.

"If such is the case, there are legal ways of procedure. But where there is one instance of such a perversion of sentimentality there are a 1,000 cases of sane and rational devotion to a dog which testify to a certain nobility in human nature, for in the love which man has for these animals, recognized since time immemorial as his greatest friend, we see evidence of the kinship of man and beast and the handiwork of the Omnipotent Creator."

With that off the editor's chest, all was quiet and the only news of victimized pets was in January 1938. "Poisoning of dogs in the city lately has aroused considerable feeling. Dog poisoners are operating again in this community and the loss of a number of these pets has occurred, while others have been saved by prompt application of remedies obtained at local drug stores and injected with a hypodermic needle.

"Contents of poisoned dogs' stomachs seem to indicate that they were given hamburger in which strychnine had been placed. Also there seems to be evidence that the poison is tossed to the dog from an automobile," the Acantha reported.

Again it was quiet, but in April 1940, after the Acantha had changed hands, Editor Karl Bishop wrote on the front page, "Decrease noted in dog population. The periodic and usually fatal epidemic that occurs every so often in the canine population of Choteau seems to be at hand again with the poisoning of one and the disappearance of two other family pets within the past week.

"One who would deliberately poison a dumb animal possesses qualities in his character that one would hesitate to admit lay in the human makeup.

"In this case, the person responsible is evidently distinctly allergic to printer's ink, as all three dogs belonged to members of that profession.

"Last week M.S. Bullerdick had the misfortune to lose his dog by poisoning. This week the black spaniel pups belonging to Howard Cunningham and Karl Bishop turned up missing and one can only conjecture as to their fate.

"If poisoned or shot, an anonymous letter would be appreciated telling where the bodies may be located — a signed letter would be even more thoroughly appreciated. If merely lost or strayed a reward is offered for information as to their whereabouts."

Dog poisoning happened on a regular basis after that. In April 1941 someone poisoned 12 dogs in Augusta. In July D.W. Hutchinson offered a reward "for information leading to the arrest and conviction of the person or persons who poisoned my dog."

In April 1942, the Acantha reported, "Dog owners of Choteau should take notice of the fact that the annual epidemic of dog poisoning is again at hand, with four local pets being poisoned in the last few days, according to reports. It seems that every spring several cases of dog poisoning occur in the city.

"Owners of dogs who have reported the loss of their pets are Geo. Sulgrove, Roy Anderson and 'Hammie' Wheeler. A dog belonging to Earl Yeager was reportedly poisoned but recovered."

In February 1943, first aid treatment saved the Dahlin dog, but a year later Bullerdick, after a spate of dog deaths declared war on "the contemptible, rotten, cowardly, despicable" dog poisoner.

As spring arrived in Choteau in 1944, the dog killings began again, and Acantha publisher Millard Bullerdick put his outrage into words.

Bullerdick had bought the Choteau Acantha in September 1942, in the midst of a world war. Rationing, war bonds and the work of the Civilian Defense Corps were important newsmakers. So was the Choteau Lions Club that held its Days of '49 fundraiser for the swimming pool. Bullerdick wrote about the men and women in uniform in 1944 along with a report that the Teton Memorial Hospital Association had filed its incorporation papers. The community began to raise funds to aid in the post-war construction of the hospital.

But in March 1944, in his column, "Your corner and mine. Culled, contributed and concocted by the editor and his friends and non-friends," he wrote extensively about the town's serial dog killer.

"The Dog poisoner — There is an old western saying which runs something like this: 'Hanging is too good for him.' An awful harsh statement, no doubt, but chock full of invective and as vitriolic as they make 'em.

"But when the old time westerner seasoned and punctuated his assertion with four short words of profanity — the first three of which are just common everyday words — well, you can bet your sweet life that there was real earnestness in the man's heart and a goodly sum of righteous indignation.

"One is tempted to use the same expressions in this supposedly more genteel age, when one hears of the contemptible, rotten, cowardly, despicable work of a dog poisoner. And one of these creatures that is a cross between rattlesnake and a jackal (with apologies to both of these animals) appears to be at work again in Choteau. On Tuesday four or five pet dogs of well-known families got hold of the vile potion and died in agony. These families included Ray Davidson, Bud Taylor, Dr. D.H Schmidt, Earl Yeager and

A.C. Hanusa.

"In speaking to the Acantha about it, one of the men said, 'If only the perpetrator of the crime could see the look on the children's faces when they learned that their pet dog was dead or when they saw it dying, perhaps it would touch their cruel heart.' To which we were forced to reply: 'It would be more practical if a two-by-four club was applied to their brazen heads.' Yes, we saw some children once gathered around a poisoned dog and every one of them was a veritable chorus of 'And he was such a good dog!'

"It was only about a year ago that one of Choteau's leading citizens offered to pay a reward of $25 for information that would lead to the arrest and conviction of a dog poisoner then at large. And he went to the trouble of getting out a leaflet on the matter and having the same distributed. This we recall as a bit of additional evidence of the genuineness and sincerity of many an adult's convictions on the matter.

"But as it is probable that Choteau and all other towns will always have some of these degraded specimens of humanity, it may be more practicable to cease denouncing and get on with some works or advice or suggestions on how best to treat a dog or what first aid can be given in an effort to save its life. Since the above was written, the toll of dog life has mounted and the statement is made that not less than 15 have died."

Bullerdick described a new effort to offer a $300 reward for information led by ex-Mayor K.E. Sturgis, who owned a hardware and automotive parts store.

"Judging from the tone of discussions in homes, in clubs, on street corners and by the public generally, it might be healthy for the perpetrator of the cowardly and dastardly act to leave the town or community 'while the leaving is good,'" Bullerdick wrote.

Sturgis's remedy: "If you find a dog poisoned, don't move him any more than necessary. The recommended antidotes are — Make him vomit immediately. Give warm lard or warm water with a one-quarter teaspoon of mustard. If apo-morphine is available, have your doctor give injection according to weight. But keep working on them until they vomit."

Mrs. J.W. Breen, who corresponded regularly for the Acantha and for the Great Falls Tribune, on March 9, 1944, wrote about the death of "Rowdy" and the serial dog killer in town.

"Rowdy, a black wool dog, lacking a pedigree except for the one he established for himself through his devotion to all children who passed the Standard Service station where he was always on the watch for cars in the event a child was crossing the street, is dead — one of the victims of the malicious person whose favorite sport appears to be to distribute poison to kill children's pets.

"Rowdy has been seen to block the way of a child on a tricycle until a car passed and to hold gently to a child's clothes to avoid the hazard of an approaching car.

"Owned by Mr. and Mrs. Ray Davidson, the dog was placed to guard the Davidson baby in the yard and the parents felt fully assured that the child would be safe. Once when he accompanied Mrs. Davidson downtown, he almost crashed through a store window when he saw a clerk pick up the child and he figured that he should come to the child's rescue.

"There are many more children mourning the loss of their pets, but this evidently doesn't worry the culprit."

By August 1944, the Acantha was calling the incidents of dog poisoning an epidemic. "The evidence reveals that the poison is strychnine and that the perpetrator or perpetrators of the crime is an 'expert' in the application and dosage of it. Where it is being obtained is not yet known, yet there seems some grounds for the assumption or belief that it comes via the gopher poison route wherein strychnine is the active ingredient," Bullerdick wrote.

He said the city and the county should be more active in investigating the incidents, and he added that the town's reputation was at stake. "To have it widely known that practically no one can keep a pet dog or a valuable dog in Choteau is certainly not to the best interest of the town in a business sense or from a social or educational angle.

"Monday evening about 6:30 the little folk in Burr Huffman's family lost their little toy terrier, 'Pepper', right while Mr. Huffman was working on a car in an alley adjacent to his home. It was pathetic to see the expression on these children's faces, as the little dog was quite a part and parcel of their young lives. And every child psychologist points out that children should have pets to promote their normal growth and development.

"Then we have numerous elderly or aging people in our town as all towns have, that have lost their kinfolk and other circumstances cause them to live alone. They find comfort and companionship in a dog. Shall it be known far and wide that Choteau is no place where such a companionship between a dog and a human can exist? ... One citizen said this week that if a few hogs or cows or sheep were poisoned, there would be official action and investigation forthwith, but when it comes to dogs — well, that's different."

Bullerdick offered to contribute to a new reward fund to "work to the end that the dastardly practice be stopped." He added, "Let's have some action in this matter right away! Mayor H.D. Robison states that the city is planning to have certain alleys in the city patrolled night and day. Let that be done. But definite sleuthing action, plus a substantial reward is an absolutely necessary adjunct as this paper sees it!"

Tom Liscum and family lost their pet dog, a female Cocker Spaniel in November, and Tom Moore offered a reward for information on who killed his children's dog in March 1945. Jack Kraft lost his dog in May 1945. By October 1946, the Acantha's new owner Jere Coffey was on the case, reporting on three dogs that were poisoned and more rewards were offered to no avail.

The town of Fairfield was also affected, according to correspondent Mrs. Melvin Bueling. "The community has two very vicious people at work. One a dog poisoner and one is a poison pen writer. As to which is the meanest I would say it was a draw and leave the decision up to their judge," she said.

In September 1948 citizens put up a $200 reward after someone poisoned six pets, during a "siege of poisonings."

The owners included the Rev. H.L. Engdahl, Joe Briscoe, Jake Zier, Jack Cherry, Billy Howard and Bud Taylor. Their dogs died, but Ed Cline's and Jere Coffey's dogs survived. Someone salted hamburger meat and left it in alleys.

Taylor offered a clue a month later when he "heard dogs growling late Sunday night, when a prowler or prowlers apparently were in the neighborhood. Next morning the dog owned by Harold Depner, who lives next door, was dead. The dog poisoner must have boldly entered the premises, it is surmised," the Acantha reported. More than 12 dogs died in the 1948 "siege."

In May 1952 "Cito," a three-year-old German shepherd police dog owned by Dr. Robert S. Hamilton of Choteau, was found dead on a Monday morning on the clinic lawn.

"The dog, which was a revered children's pet, left the clinic about 5 a.m. and lay dead on the lawn when discovered at 8 o'clock. Dog poisoning particularly is dangerous for children who may pick up poisonous objects which could lead to human death," the Acantha stated.

The incident prompted Ruth Holt's letter to the editor, "Someone has decided to plant Death in Choteau. The first object of this person is to avenge himself on dogs. The second is to place the lives of small children in danger."

She added, "It is very difficult for the normal person, whether he is a dog lover or whether dogs bother him, to imagine the lengths to which our neighbor has gone. Even those who were most anxious to have the new and controversial dog ordinance passed are revolted by a dog poisoner."

She said the dog problem rested with the city and its enforcement. "No one has the right to destroy valuable property belonging to another. ... If we tried to take upon ourselves the elimination of all the aggravations that beset us in a lifetime, I'm afraid the population, animal and human, would soon be gone. Everyone has a pet peeve. If everyone exercised his primitive selfish instincts, we might as well forget about all the years of civilization ...," she said.

In the spring of 1953, a report noted, "Last Wednesday night a registered Boxer owned by Benny Chalmers of Choteau was killed in front of his house, located on the west side of the city near the Hensley Motel. The dog, which had been a boy's Christmas present last Christmas Day, died immediately in front of the Chalmers house only 20 minutes after the animal had been let out of the house.

"A collie dog in the same neighborhood, owned by Harry Luinstra, died of poisoning the same night.

"Chalmers took the remains of his pet to Helena for inspection by the state livestock sanitary board, from which he soon expects to receive a report. He said the poison was a vicious, fast-working type — possibly strychnine or 10-80. The latter is a very potent mixture put out by the federal government only for federal use in this area for coyote kill."

In April 1954, the Acantha said Dale Anderson's bird

dog, a German shepherd short-haired pointer, was found poisoned near the honey factory building on the south side.

In December 1957 Jim Dellwo's beagle dog was found poisoned on a Tuesday morning. The animal had made his way to the Dellwo's front step when it collapsed. Police Chief Maurice Black said another dog was found poisoned the same day in the area near the high school. Black said a total of four dogs had been poisoned recently.

However, sympathy for dogs running at large had its limits as the old newspaper reports reveal. An overpopulation of unleashed, unvaccinated dogs became a chronic problem.

In 1925, a dog traced to Choteau bit eight dogs while the unnamed owner traveled with it to Great Falls. One of those dogs bit a young girl who died of rabies. A lab report on the Choteau dog's head proved positive for the scary disease.

The city council's reaction was a campaign for an emergency dog ordinance including a leash law and summary destruction of unvaccinated, unlicensed stray dogs. After that, each time the council took up the topic over the following decades, the controversy split the community, but that's another story.

1963

June 19, 2013

Ask any Choteau area baby boomer or septuagenarian what they remember from the early 1960s, before the June 1964 flood that would dominate the decade, and many might say Pres. J.F. Kennedy's assassination, while people familiar with Main Avenue might mention the mini-building boom.

Fifty years ago, Zion Construction demolished the old Monarch Lumber building, built in 1912, and the former St. Anthony and Dakota yard, to make room for two new stores.

Teton Furniture had its grand opening in July 1963. Next to it were the Villager hardware store and the Tree Top Restaurant on the second floor, now the Choteau/Teton Public Library of today. The old furniture store building was the Bridges Coffee House for a short while.

The old lumberyard appears in all the old photos taken from the second floor windows of the Teton County Courthouse.

The new buildings were the first extensive construction on Main in a number of years.

In keeping with the upbeat climate, the Choteau Chamber of Commerce in July hosted a Choteau Appreciation Day and served 1,000 people a free lunch, among other things.

Business leaders celebrated the expansion of Lee's Grocery, the opening of a new $30,000 federal office building (where the New Song Church is now) and looked forward to the Choteau House becoming a bar and steakhouse on Main, it having been a mix of businesses before then, including the Choteau Bar, Joe's Barbershop, Choteau Shoe Repair and the Penguin Cafe.

They worried when a blaze razed the Gallatin Valley Grain Elevator in September at the same site of one that burned in July 1953, and they fretted over a long running controversy over bar closing hours.

Choteau not only got direct long-distance dialing later in 1963, but also got a Zip Code.

But other things stayed the same. A chinook wind raised the temperature from 16 below zero to 51 degrees between a Saturday and Sunday in February, melting eight inches of snow. It was the most effective chinook since 1912, said an old timer. January was said to be the coldest month in many years, it being below zero for 16 nights, with the lowest temperature having reached 31 below zero on Jan. 22.

In a countywide campaign children and adults got the oral Sabin vaccine (three for kids and two for adults) for $.25 per dose to protect them from polio but no one could protect them from the memory and the shock when Kennedy died on Nov. 22. More than 750 people attended a memorial service in the Choteau High School gym.

Index

www.ingramcontent.com/pod-product-compliance
Lightning Source LLC
Chambersburg PA
CBHW021051090426
42738CB00006B/290